ASTROLOGY AND ANTHROPOSOPHY

RON ODAMA

B&H Bennett & Hastings Publishing

ACKNOWLEDGEMENTS

I would like to thank my wife, Marilyn, for her encouragement. Without it, I may not have completed the writing of this book. She, along with my children and students, whose lives it has been a pleasure to watch unfold and validate the study of astrology.

I am grateful, as well, for the help of the teachers and mentors who have guided me along the way, and I am very thankful for Rudolf Steiner and anthroposophy for giving me inspiration in my work at the Waldorf Schools and in writing this book.

CONTENTS

Notations: Signs of the Zodiac

Aries	♈	Cancer	♋	Libra	♎	Capricorn	♑
Taurus	♉	Leo	♌	Scorpio	♏	Aquarius	♒
Gemini	♊	Virgo	♍	Sagittarius	♐	Pisces	♓

INTRODUCTION

My love of astrology comes from an appreciation of the wisdom I have been able to draw from an understanding of myself and others. It has been a lifelong task that continues. In this book I hope to share with you my methods and notes on how to interpret natal astrology charts with the methodology I use. At the end of the book I will give you a practical example – my own chart. I hope this autobiography helps the reader in understanding how to apply my methodology of natal chart reading. All of the keys are there if contemplated.

In 1942, shortly after Pearl Harbor was bombed, my parents – along with 120,000 other west coast Japanese Americans – were evacuated from the coastal states and sent further inland to concentration camps. This was a governmental response to war hysteria fueled by fear that Japanese Americans were a security threat. The internees did not know their fate nor what would be the duration of their confinement. They lived in fear, punished for crimes they had not committed. They were judged by the United States federal government and suffered discrimination based on their easily distinguishable racial characteristics. They lost their businesses, real estate, possessions and years as free citizens. They were deprived of their hopes and dreams. They were suspended in time and forced to adjust to their fate. I was born into that environment in the Amache, Colorado internment camp. Obviously, my soul development needed that beginning.

In 1945, after World War II ended, my family was sent by train back to Lomita, California to live in government housing. We stayed there only one day, because I could not breathe the atmosphere: my asthma was so serious that the authorities sent us to better housing in Long Beach, California. At age forty-one, my father had to start life over again. He somehow got an old push mower and began a gardening business. He had to walk his route. Before the war he owned a produce stand in North Hollywood, but now he had no capital. My parents had always valued education, and their emphasis on it increased greatly after their wartime experience. They instilled this value in their children. We were taught that we had to be better than all other people to prove our worthiness as citizens. I think this distinguished the mainland Japanese from the Hawaiian Japanese, who had not been evacuated during the war. When I started kindergarten my mother went to work in fish canning factories on Terminal Island. She worked long hours and rose to become a manager. She learned to speak Spanish fluently, adding that language to her mastery of English and Japanese. She retained Japanese cultural values in her love of nature, art, music and Zen. She always considered herself an artist. As a teenager, after graduating from Pasadena High School she had spent one year at the Pasadena Art Institute before economic necessity led her to quit and become a secretary. Later, she became an accomplished sumie painter, and writer of haiku. My father was of the first generation, or Issei; Japanese citizens who came to America for work. He had a good education in Japan, but he was hampered by the language after coming to America at age fifteen.

When I went to college I was caught up in the hysteria of the nation as we tried to compete with the Soviet Union in science and technology after Sputnik. I studied mechanical engineering even though I had no aptitude nor interest in it. My goal was to get my degree and become a respectable engineer. I was living subservient to perceived expectations placed upon me. I was caught up in the materialistic values of a "good" life. I worked as a mechanical/aerospace engineer for six years and surrounded myself with status symbol possessions. I found them to bring me emptiness of soul. I was always fortunate to have good older people as mentors. Leaving on my birthday in 1971, I went to Europe with friends. We traveled there in a VW van for eight months, and I discovered my own natural rhythms and instincts while gaining perspective on other people's values and lifestyles. Europeans' values had a deep impact on me: people were community-focused, relished good food and drink and believed life should be enjoyed. I could see how I had been manipulated by capitalism and its time structures, products and systems of control. I was determined to find my own interests and vocation and at the same time integrate myself as a more productive member of society. It was the time of the Civil Rights movement, Viet Nam War, civil disobedience, flower power, drugs, Women's Liberation, and birth control.

When I returned to Los Angeles I was determined to go back to school in a more humanistic and spiritualized course of study. I chose to study psychology and astrology. I found my perfect partner and was married in 1973 at my Saturn return. Upon returning from our honeymoon I went to work on a construction job making steel silencing containers for jet engines used to generate electricity. I was there for one hour when a steel door slammed shut in an "accident," and I lost the tips of three fingers on my right hand. I recognized that I had a karmic relationship with the owner of the company, the brother of my stock broker. In a previous life he had lived as a woman, and I had carelessly cut her fingers with my sword.

While I was recuperating, I decided to become a Special Education teacher and help children in need of special care. I was again fortunate to have excellent mentors among my professors and thesis advisors. While attending school, I worked for the Los Angeles Public School system as a teaching assistant in a junior high school. The students there were all African-Americans, and I learned a lot about their racial group. After completing my degree I went to work teaching English as a Second Language to refugees from the Indochinese War; Korean and Filipino immigrants. These experiences allowed me to explore my own prejudices and discover our common humanity along with our differences.

At this time I began to study Anthroposophy in a study group hosted by my mentor, Clark Done. I then found the Waldorf School teacher training program[1] at Highland Hall in Los Angeles. I enrolled and found another mentor in Virginia Sease. After completing my course of study I went to work as a Waldorf teacher at the Denver Waldorf School while being mentored by Lyman Jackson. While there another experienced teacher, Bill Bryant, came to be my mentor. After two years, we left to start a Waldorf School in South Dakota to be free of political differences. I found that it was not easy to gain philosophical support in conservative thinking environments. Financial hardships forced the teachers

---

1   The Waldorf School and its curriculum was designed by Rudolf Steiner, the founder of Anthroposophy. The purpose was to age-appropriately bring the principles of Anthroposophy into formal education.

to abandon Waldorf education principles in deference to pragmatism. I didn't agree with this compromise.

I went to teach Special Education on the Pine Ridge Reservation in Kyle, South Dakota, working with Lakota children. I was determined to apply Waldorf principles and techniques in my teaching and to seek potential teachers who could pursue a Waldorf teacher training degree and return to the reservation. Twenty-four years later I found that I had been successful, to my great happiness. I wish the best for the Waldorf School initiative in Kyle.

After two years I went back to teach in the public school system at Ellsworth Air Force Base in South Dakota. I worked with children of the Air Force families, who were of varied racial backgrounds.

When it became time for my wife and I to find a Waldorf school for our own children, our search led us to Portland, Oregon. There we found a Waldorf school where I could teach and our children attend. I would teach there several years, taking a class from third grade through their eighth grade graduation. It was a very satisfying experience and another pioneering school effort. Teaching the Waldorf curriculum while incorporating Anthroposophy as a background for inspiration was of great benefit to me. The result was a reworking of my own education while teaching my young students. I took my graduating class to Europe for three weeks, me being the only adult. We travelled without mishap. The only prearranged reservation we had was the ferry boat reservation from Italy to Greece. We all learned to trust in the future. I still feel very connected to this core group of students, even after twenty years.

Upon returning I went to work as an insurance agent/financial planner for Prudential Insurance. Again, I had the benefit of good mentors. I was successful but didn't enjoy my attempt at working in business. I wanted to teach in the Waldorf schools. I found a position in Kona, Hawaii, and we moved our family to the birth island of my wife. I felt my destiny was to teach Hawaiian and Asian children. Instead, most of my students were Caucasian. Their families could be described as refugees from the mainland. Most were hooked on marijuana and promises were not kept regarding support. And after four years of living in paradise we left to teach in Seattle. I was forced out due to political differences and then spent three years teaching Special Education in the public schools. I was dismayed to find that there was no discipline enforced due to fear of lawsuits by parents. Education had turned to babysitting. I was "Old School." My last teaching attempt was to teach at a Waldorf school in Bellevue, Washington. To my dismay I found that the Waldorf school was not following Rudolf Steiner's indications but was a pragmatic school without Anthroposophy. The teachers did not study and were finding their own educational inspirations.

After my kidneys began to fail, I retired and began to devote my time to astrology and this book. I thank everyone who supported me in making this book possible.

Principles of Spiritual Astrology

All the world's a stage,
And all the men and women merely players;
They have their exits and entrances;
And one man in his time plays many parts,
His acts being seven ages …"

(As You Like It; II VII) Shakespeare

Astrological Chart – A map of the soul's revelation as it unfolds in consciousness through the element of time. Higher spiritual beings reveal their influence, in ebb and flow, through the movement of the planets with stars and constellations as backdrop. Man's purpose is to return to God, overcoming karma through growth in consciousness under the Law of Grace, a force for karmic redemption without one-to-one retribution. Man is to experience love and brotherhood while overcoming the self in freedom. He must choose each day to follow the Christ path between Lucifer/light and Ahriman/darkness[1].

Microcosm/Macrocosm Correspondence – "As above, so below." Each individual must become the center of his own consciousness, just as the Sun is the center of the solar system. Human beings are connected with the cosmos, i.e. each person's endocrine glands are correlated to the planets. All material manifestations are reflections of the spirit.

Reincarnation and Karma – We were once perfect spiritual beings but have become enmeshed in the earth planet due to our karma. This happened after the Fall from Paradise. We seek a return to God as perfected soul beings. To do this we must cleanse our souls, in freedom, to align ourselves with the Christ path by choosing Love and earning the law of Grace through greater consciousness.

---

1   See Appendix: Two Faces of Evil.

ZODIAC – has its center in the individual self. The constellations are the circumference of spiritual beings. Planets are the focalizers of spiritual forces of the zodiac.

NOTATIONS: SIGNS OF THE ZODIAC

Aries	♈	Cancer	♋	Libra	♎	Capricorn	♑
Taurus	♉	Leo	♌	Scorpio	♏	Aquarius	♒
Gemini	♊	Virgo	♍	Sagittarius	♐	Pisces	♓

FORCE MANIFESTING IN MATTER AND SPIRIT MANIFESTING IN FORM

$$\begin{array}{r} 4 \\ \times\,3 \\ \hline 12 \end{array}$$

ELEMENTS – earth, air, fire, water
CROSSES – thinking, feeling, willing[2]
SIGNS – cardinal, fixed, mutable; will, love, wisdom

FOUR ELEMENTS	SIGNS			TEMPERAMENTS – CARL JUNG
	CARDINAL	FIXED	MUTABLE	
Fire	♈ Aries	♌ Leo	♐ Sagittarius	Choleric – Intuition
Air	♎ Libra	♒ Aquarius	♊ Gemini	Sanguine – Thinking
Water	♋ Cancer	♏ Scorpio	♓ Pisces	Phlegmatic – Feeling
Earth	♑ Capricorn	♉ Taurus	♍ Virgo	Melancholic – Sensation
SOUL EXPRESSION:	WILL	LOVE	WISDOM	

TRIPLICITIES AND QUADRUPLICITIES

FIRE, AIR, WATER, EARTH: TRIPLICITIES – The three signs in any single element form a triplicity and resultant characteristics, noted above. Aries, Leo, Sagittarius form a triplicity in the element of fire.

CARDINAL, FIXED, MUTABLE: QUADRUPLICITIES – The four cardinal signs tend to initiate activity and take charge. The four fixed signs tend to be tenacious and enjoy stability. The four mutable signs tend towards change and exhibit adaptability.

ANGULAR, SUCCEEDENT, CADENT: QUADRUPLICITIES – The four angular houses are characterized by beginnings, the four succeedent houses by progress and the four cadent houses by endings. (See also p. 26.)

---

2   More on this threefold soul expression in the Appendix.

THE TEMPERAMENTS – The temperaments are studied in the natal chart by looking at the houses. The rising sign generally indicates the physical characteristics of the temperament, but not always. It can be a mixture of influences coming from the sun, moon, planets of emphasis, etc. The persona or personality projection is greatly influenced by the rising sign as the mask used by the individuality to affect its environment. The temperaments have been studied since ancient Greece to understand the individual and to treat them accordingly for best education and personal relations. Rudolf Steiner advocates their use in the Waldorf schools to facilitate classroom management and to promote educational efficiency through cooperative learning. I think it is helpful to recognize temperamental traits in helping to understand and advise clients. Therefore, I will give a brief description of each of the four temperaments and how to lovingly handle them[3].

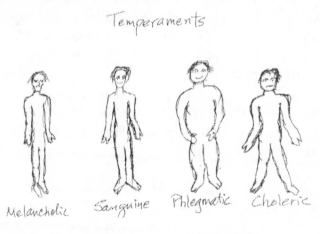

Temperaments

Melancholic   Sanguine   Phlegmatic   Choleric

MELANCHOLIC	SANGUINE	PHLEGMATIC	CHOLERIC
blue	yellow	green	red
lanky, bony	well proportioned	rounded	short, compact
stooped, thoughtful	light footed	good disposition	energetic
Physical body	Astral Body	Etheric Body	Ego Body
Past	Present	Present	Future
thinkers	movie stars	stewards	leaders

---

3   More notes on this topic can be found in the Appendix.

THE MELANCHOLIC

The Melancholic temperament is characterized by a serious outlook on life. They look into the past with a historic perspective. Pain and suffering and the adjustment to the trials of life's experiences color their outlook. They are introverts and can become too self-concerned with worries and anxieties about things that never happen. They want to be prepared for the worst. They can be hypochondriacs, have phobias, and have health, nutrition and cleanliness issues. They have a need to be convinced to take action because of their hesitancy. They can be tyrants, ruling their household from their sickbeds. They may create situations where they create pain and suffering for others. Physically, they are slender, tall, and stooped. They appear to be carrying the weight of the world on their backs. Their color is dark with dark wispy straight hair. They don't feel comfortable in their bodies as their limbs do not do what the thinking says. They can be clumsy and inept at doing things with their hands. They can plan well with attention to details but may be myopic in view. They can tell their stories of woe ad nauseam. Because of their seriousness they can be found in the medical and service professions. They make excellent writers, novelists, and poets. When young they thrive on stories of real life adventures when challenges were met and overcome. They must never be allowed to be overcome with their fears.

THE SANGUINE

The Sanguine temperament is characterized by a light, non-serious outlook on life. They are the opposite temperament to the Melancholic. They live in the present with a happy-go-lucky attitude. They are extroverts and thrust themselves into life's experiences. They have a zest for life and have fun. The danger is they may be superficial and lack depth of insight into life's experiences. One can't be a butterfly and just touch the flowers. Physically, the Sanguine is beautiful, well formed, slender, and graceful with the look of a Greek statue with its generic look. They are very light on their feet. The hair is blonde or light brown with blue or hazel eyes. Hollywood is filled with aspiring Sanguines. They have a knack for language and conversation, and they learn by listening. They make excellent news reporters and commentators. They do not report in depth because they are always ready to go on to the next topic. Interests are always changing – they are drawn to the new – so they are interested in fashion, beauty, cosmetics, hair styles, the arts and music. They love uniforms and may be drawn to armed forces, police forces, fire fighting, etc., where they can be semi-autonomous. They do not like to stand out as individuals. In fact, they seek Cholerics to follow since Cholerics are not as impressionable. Sanguines like to test through criticism to find Cholerics who do not respond to them: they can then rely on them and follow their lead. Sanguines' great danger is to lose control of the ego and to lose their integrity. If pressured, they will lie and make excuses. In love affairs, they seek a type of personality and have trouble distinguishing the individuality.

THE PHLEGMATIC

The Phlegmatic temperament is characterized by an easygoing outlook and the search for comfort. They wish to be self-contained and be left alone, as they live in the present. They love stability and routine. They are not talkative and sociable. They are methodical. They can be satisfied with doing the same tasks over and over for years. Give them something to imitate and then, to make them happy in their heart of hearts, something on which they can make some innovation. If you need to correct them in their work, make corrections without comment and leave them alone. Physically, they can be likened to a well padded easy chair. They are large, fleshy and rounded with a digestive system that predominates. They can be relatively light on their feet and not clumsy. They love food and can make excellent cooks. They must make an effort to try new ideas and things. They gain interests from observing what interests others. They can be cultivated to approve of something new by building familiarity and emphasizing both its acceptability to socially prominent people and its quality and endurance. They make excellent accountants and bankers, because they neither make snap decisions nor act on rumors and fads. They are attracted to Sanguines, who have traits that they lack. Their greatest danger is to become inactive, dull and disinterested in life beyond themselves.

THE CHOLERIC

The Choleric temperament is characterized by an intense, masterful outlook and a search for challenges to overcome. They live in the future and contemplate what they will bend to their will. They are not impressionable but can be rigid in their demands of themselves and of others. They are the born leaders but must learn to respect the opinions and abilities of others. If they are allowed, they can become megalomaniacs, and must be balanced by the group. Appeal must be made to their sense of justice and to see the harm they have done to others. They can't resist helping those in need and can become great benefactors. They are developing a social sense. Physically, they are short, muscular, and exude energy. They seem to look down their noses at you and appear larger than they are. They make good leaders and managers because they can organize and get things done. Since their egos are strong, they can't stand to be compared to others. They are quick to anger and must watch their high blood pressure. Their greatest danger is to overestimate themselves and underestimate others.

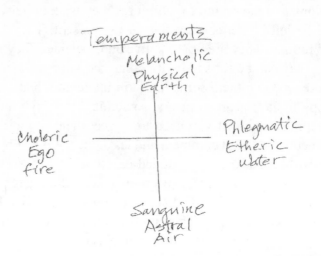

Which temperament is missing in the persona? This indicates over development in past lives.

SOUL LEVELS – To better interpret astrological charts it is necessary to determine at what soul level the subject is living. The three soul levels are (1) Sentient Soul, (2) Intellectual or Mind Soul, and (3) Consciousness or Spiritual Soul. Here I present just the basic concepts of the soul levels. I will present more detailed information in the next chapter.

SENTIENT SOUL

The individual thinks, feels, and acts driven by selfish passions, desires, likes and dislikes, and sensations and is struggling to gain control of impulses.

INTELLECTUAL OR MIND SOUL

The individual thinks, feels and acts driven by intellectual reasoning, cause and effect references, rigid adherence to laws and rules (letter of the law), logic and rhetoric to make judgments.

CONSCIOUSNESS OR SPIRITUAL SOUL

The individual thinks, feels, and acts driven by the need to consider the common good, applying wisdom to judgment (spirit of the law) and seeking spiritual guidance. There is an understanding of the value of rules and laws but there is also the desire to apply them on an individual basis.

There is a maturation process towards the Consciousness Soul that characterizes the historical development of humankind, as there is in the life of each individual. The most primitive cultures developed the Sentient Soul, the Intellectual Soul was developed during the Greco-Roman period, and the Consciousness Soul has been developing since the Renaissance. In the individual life the ego must experience itself through the Sentient Soul at 21 years, the Intellectual Soul at 28 years, and the Consciousness Soul at 35 years. Of course these transitions are not always exact but are processes in potential. And we do not always manage to operate at our highest soul level.

In chart reading it is helpful to visualize the soul levels as a spiral arising three dimensionally from the chart to indicate at which level the planetary aspects can be interpreted. The higher the soul level the more freedom from karmic consequences.

CHART RULER – The chart ruler is determined by finding the sign on the Ascendant (the rising sign at the time of your birth) and determining *its ruling planet*. (See chart on next page.) This is the chart ruler. It is important in finding the focus of the chart as it has locomotive force for the will to express the persona.

PLANETARY RULERSHIP

NOTATIONS		RULES SIGN/HOUSE		DETRIMENT SIGN/HOUSE		EXALTATION/FALL
☉	Sun	♌ Leo	5	♒ Aquarius	11	♈ Aries / ♎ Libra
☽	Moon	♋ Cancer	4	♑ Capricorn	10	♉ Taurus / ♏ Scorpio
☿	Mercury	♊ Gemini ♍ Virgo	3 6	♐ Sagittarius ♓ Pisces	9 12	♍ Virgo / ♓ Pisces
♀	Venus	♉ Taurus ♎ Libra	2 7	♏ Scorpio ♈ Aries	8 1	♓ Pisces / ♍ Virgo
♂	Mars	♈ Aries	1	♎ Libra	7	♑ Capricorn / ♋ Cancer
♃	Jupiter	♐ Sagittarius	9	♊ Gemini	3	♋ Cancer / ♑ Capricorn
♄	Saturn	♑ Capricorn	10	♋ Cancer	4	♎ Libra / ♈ Aries
♅	Uranus	♒ Aquarius	11	♌ Leo	5	♏ Scorpio / ♉ Taurus
♆	Neptune	♓ Pisces	12	♍ Virgo	6	♋ Cancer / ♑ Capricorn
♇	Pluto	♏ Scorpio	8	♉ Taurus	2	♓ Pisces / ♍ Virgo

PLANETARY PATTERNS – I have found that in looking at the Natal Chart it is helpful to determine the basic planetary pattern configuration. I refer the reader to the work of Marc Edmund Jones and his book *The Guide to Horoscope Interpretation* (Sabian Publishing Society) for a full explanation of his method and delineation. Marc Edmund Jones calls this "the method of whole view." I only touch on some basic patterns as a quick explanation. It is also important to study the patterns to see the importance of focal planets indicated by the planetary patterns. Only the ten planets are considered in the determination of the planetary pattern.

THE SPLASH TYPE

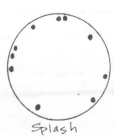

Splash

In this planetary pattern all of the planets are distributed more or less evenly around the chart. This pattern indicates that the subject can develop wholistic philosophical viewpoints or can become scattered. Examples are Jacob Bohme, Emmanuel Kant, and Richard Wagner, Theodore Roosevelt, and Leon Trotsky according to Jones.

THE BUNDLE TYPE

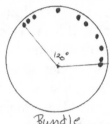

Bundle

The Bundle pattern has all of the planets clustered within the span of a trine. This pattern indicates a personality that is very much self contained with its own inertia that operates by sheer opportunism, reacting to what is at hand. Like a spinning top, it throws off all challenges and soon rights itself. Examples are Mussolini, William James, and William McKinley.

THE LOCOMOTIVE TYPE

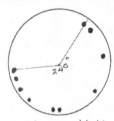

Locomotive

This planetary pattern is the opposite of the Bundle in that all planets are found in a span of two hundred and forty degrees. The leading planet is the following planet of the missing trine as seen scooping out experience in the clockwise direction. It indicates a personality that either has a strong sense of need or a lack of need of a problem to be solved found in the social and intellectual world around him/her. It is a self driving individuality in a real practical sense to be activated. The outstanding example of this pattern is Sir Isaac Newton who in solitude in his twenty fourth year produced his Three Laws of Motion and the accompanying mathematics (calculus) to define them. Other examples are George Washington, Mary Baker Eddy, George Gershwin, Cecil Rhodes and Upton Sinclair.

THE BOWL TYPE

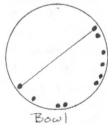

Bowl

This pattern indicates a hemispheric emphasis that seems to contain or bear some burden. The leading planet is at the rim of the bowl scooping out experience in the clockwise direction. Note if there is a defining opposition on the rim or a T cross. This gives the personality defining strength. It is as if the individual feels set off from the rest of the world and wants to experience it. The Bowl personality must rely on hi/her own sense of values to react to what is found coming from experience. Examples are Abraham Lincoln, Oliver Cromwell, Helen Keller, Frederic Chopin, and Edgar Allen Poe.

THE BUCKET TYPE

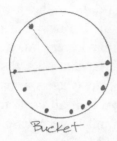

Bucket

This pattern is similar to the Bowl pattern except that in opposition to the Bowl is a singleton planet or a conjunction of two planets. This handle of the bucket is a focal determinator indicating a special capacity or gift some particularly effective kind of activity. Jones indicates that when the handle is located between the rim and the vertical position life tends toward caution and self-conscious preparedness. If the handle is located between the vertical and the other rim, the life is more impulsive or reactionary.

The Bucket personality can be the excellent instructor and motivator or the malcontent and agitator. The Bucket individual goes deeply and focuses resources with great energy.

The outstanding example of this type is Napoleon Bonaparte who personified the modern day Caesar with kingly aplomb. He was an excellent proponent of the use of artillery in warfare, using the latest technology and education, gave the Napoleonic Code of Laws, established the metric system of measurement, and sent his scientists to rediscover the Egyptian roots of civilization. Other examples of the Bucket type are Dante, Lewis Carroll, and George Bernard Shaw.

THE SEESAW TYPE

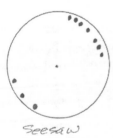

Seesaw

This pattern is characterized by two roughly opposite groupings of planets. As the name implies this temperament attempts to keep a balance between opposing views and choices of action. The outstanding example is Percy Bysshe Shelley the romantic poet and social reformer rebelling against intellectualism and social norms. Other seesaw examples are Emmanuel Swedenborg, Rudyard Kipling, and Karl Marx. All were social reformers and commentators proclaiming new ways of thought.

THE SPLAY TYPE

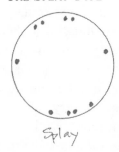

Splay

In this pattern planetary patterns are neither symmetrical nor even. This indicates a highly individual emphasis in life expression. The individual is hard to categorize and is eccentric and unpredictable. The outstanding example of this type is Henry VIII, who with his individualistic emphasis broke with the Catholic Church and ruled England with sheer opportunism and self interest including flaunting the divorce laws with his many wives. This led to the death of many of his court including Sir Thomas More. Another example of this type is Jay Gould the American financier who made millions dabbling in industry, transportation and the stock market through ruthlessness and self interest. An- other example, in a more positive vein, is Carl Jung who developed Analytic Psychology and categorized the different levels of consciousness, dreams, mandalas, and archetypes as a study of the Soul. He traveled across the globe studying native cultures and belief systems to find commonality in meaning and truth. He used his splay temperament in his diversity of interests and research while promoting the dignity of the individual.

ASPECTS – When studying aspects between planets it is important to remember that the relationship between planets begins with the conjunction and continues through all major and minor aspects between the planets and then back to the new conjunction. The progression is leading to a higher spiral of consciousness in maturity of the influence of the planets. The faster moving planet indicates whether the aspect is applying (coming into exact aspect) or separating (leaving the exact aspect). The effects of the applying aspects tend to have greater influence. For example, the closing square between planets should indicate more maturity in dealing with life events than the opening square. In order to get a better sense of this I recommend the study of the book *The Lunation Cycle: A Key to the Understanding of Personality* by Dane Rudhyar, Shambala Publications, Inc. This book is a study of the relationship between the aspects of the Sun and Moon or the Moon phases.

It is interesting to note that due to the proximity to the Sun, the personal planets Mercury and Venus can only experience the conjunction, semi-sextile and semi-square. They must be studied in their relation to rising before and after the Sun and whether direct or retrograde. It is said by some astrologers that if any planet is closely conjunct to the Sun it is combust and loses its influence, but I think it is better to think of its influence as being very subjective. Conjunctions between planets can be either harmonious or inharmonious. Saturn in conjunction tends to overrule the influence of the other planet until its usage has gained maturity. Another interesting fact is that Mars goes retrograde when it nears opposition to the Sun. How appropriate that Mars must work internally to struggle with the ego to gain maturity.

Studying the meaning and influences of the planets in the signs and houses should give you the basis to interpret the aspects between planets in synthesis. It gets a little more complicated when we encounter multiple conjunctions – but we can then appreciate the complexity of the soul of the individuality being studied. They are preparing to express a whole new level of consciousness. Any aspects, even negative aspects between planets, are better than having no aspects. Aspects indicate avenues of potential expression, growth and development of consciousness. If a planet has no aspects, it is not operating under conscious control. The maturity of the soul is indicated by the number and quality of the aspects in the natal chart.

In order to understand the effects of aspects, study the planets in the signs and houses and blend together the meanings to see if the subject is using the forces positively or negatively. If the personal planets out to Saturn are not aspected to the trans-Saturnian planets, then this indicates that the individual is concerned with the mundane concerns of everyday life and not global or humanitarian issues. Remember that in the school of life we attract the lessons we need.

The next chart lists both exact degrees of aspect and orb. Orb represents the limits of the aspect, which can vary from exact in either a plus or minus direction. Note that orb for sun and moon differs from orb for other planets, and that orb is related to the aspect strength. The closer an aspect is to being exact, the stronger the effect.

ASPECT	NOTATION	STRENGTH	EXACT	ORB (+/-) ☉☾	ORB (+/-) ALL OTHERS
CONJUNCTION	☌	MAJOR	0°	≤10°	≤ 8°
INCONJUNCTS (A.K.A. QUINCUNX)	⚻	MINOR	150°	≤4°	≤ 2°
OPPOSITIONS	☍	MAJOR	180°	≤10°	≤ 8°
QUINTILES	Q	MINOR	72°	≤10°	≤ 2°
SQUARES	□	MAJOR	90°	≤10°	≤ 8°
SEXTILES	⚹	MAJOR	60°	≤10°	≤ 8°
SEMI-SQUARES (A.K.A. SEMI-QUARTILES)	∠	MINOR	45°	≤4°	≤ 2°
SEMI-SEXTILES	⚺	MINOR	30°	≤4°	≤ 2°
SEPTILES	S	MINOR	51°	≤4°	≤ 2°
TRINES	Δ	MAJOR	120°	≤10°	≤ 8°

SUN AND MOON – Use an orb of no greater than 10 degrees from exact for conjunctions, sextiles, trines, squares, and oppositions. Use up to 4 degrees for semi-quartiles, semi-sextiles, inconjuncts, quintiles or septiles. These guidelines are summarized under the sun and moon notations in the chart above.

FOR ALL OTHER PLANETS – Use 8 degrees orb or less for MAJOR ASPECTS and 2 degrees or less for MINOR ASPECTS. This is summarized in the last column of the above chart.

QUINTILES AND SEPTILES are minor aspects that indicate talents or natural abilities or may indicate an unusual destiny to be lived.

SEMI-SEXTILES AND SEMI-SQUARES – Minor aspects need attention because we are working on them to become major aspects.

CHARTING ASPECTS – You may want to use colored and textured lines to indicate various aspects on the charts you are reading. I use the following colored ASPECT LINES between planets when I draw up a chart:

ASPECTS		COLOR I USE ON CHART
CONJUNCTION	♂	
INCONJUNCTS (A.K.A. QUINCUNX)	⚻	ORANGE
OPPOSITIONS	☍	RED
QUINTILES	Q	VIOLET
SQUARES	□	RED
SEXTILES	✳	GREEN
SEMI-SQUARES (A.K.A. SEMI-QUARTILES)	∠	DASHED RED
SEMI-SEXTILES	⊻	DASHED GREEN
SEPTILES	S	VIOLET
TRINES	Δ	BLUE

CRITICAL DEGREES – These degrees wield more power and influence.

1°, 13°, 26°	• activity • leadership	CARDINAL
9°, 21°, 15°	• will, • concentrative	FIXED
4°, 17°	• relationships • communication	MUTABLE

INTERCEPTIONS

When there are interceptions in the birth chart, there is an out of timing of space and time karma. It indicates some karmic fulfillment must be made. It indicates a defect in the consciousness. This vibratory defect brings out a consciousness of past lives and what has to be redeemed. The planets enclosed in the interceptions were misused or neglected or not properly applied in past lives. Therefore, we do not have conscious control over the powers of the planets and must be passive in regards to their usage. We must wait for opportunities to come to us through life experiences. Without being aware of it the individual is awaiting the crisis where interceptions and duplicated signs and their dispositors will be involved. The dispositors of intercepted signs are also held in abeyance until some degree of redemption has been made. Consciousness changes are occurring regarding the planets involved. The dispositors of the duplicated diameters will be working overtime to make up for lost time and opportunities for growth of consciousness. As life proceeds, a certain amount of movement, freedom and awakening of consciousness is gained. The persons do not operate creatively out of intercepted signs until the crisis is past. The lower degree cusp houses are not as important as the upper degree houses. The lower degree house can be thought of as the twelfth house of the upper degree house and must be fulfilled through the upper degree house affairs. We have a tendency to live in the affairs of the lower degree house by habit. Past life dispositions will tend to overlay this life, but we must move on.

There may be psychological disequilibrium from over development or misuse in past lives.

There may be subconscious complexes, neuroses, phobias and inhibitions and in the extreme there could be incurable illnesses and insanity involved. There can be very heavy karma if Saturn is involved with interceptions. If intercepted planets are not afflicted they may show over development relative to the soul's development. Afflicted planets show misuse.

Fate or destiny operates in the matters of the intercepted houses. If karma is redeemed a high degree of development can be accomplished. There will be much subconscious motivation to solve complexes. Time will seem to move faster when the point of self goes through the intercepted signs. There could be insulation from outside conditions as the person may be able to act totally independently from the house of the intercepted sign. The experience of this can be very subjective so it may not be noticeable to other people.

LIFE CYCLES

ASTROLOGICAL CHART AND BODY CORRESPONDENCES

What most people consider as birth is only the birth of the Physical Body because it is visible to the senses. The Etheric, or life body, is also born to the earth's forces, but is not visible to the senses. It works closely with the physical body and does not separate from it until death. A glimpse of this separation occurs at near death experiences as a memory tableau of pictures of one's life experiences. The Etheric Body is visible to more sensitive perception and is referred to as the aura. It is in continual movement and builds up and repairs the physical body in rhythmical fashion. In the birth chart it is represented by the houses with the background of the Zodiac. It is a picture also of the Temperaments as described by Rudolf Steiner. The ascendant sign of the first house gives an indication of the appearance of the Physical Body and the Persona. Usually there is a strong correspondence of the elements with the temperament, but the Sun and Moon can have a strong effect. Fire (Choleric), Earth (Melancholic), Air (Sanguine), and Water (Phlegmatic) are the basic correspondences. The time period of correspondence of the Etheric Body is seven years. It is said that every cell of the body is replaced every seven years except for brain and nervous system cells. This shows the close relationship of the Etheric and Physical Bodies.

In using the Point of Self (Dane Rudhyar) time is kept in twenty-eight year cycles with ascendant, *Imum Coeli*, descendant, and mid-heaven points as the quadrant points. Basically, we can count three of these cycles as allotted to the human life. The years twenty-eight, fifty-six and eighty-four mark the three cycles. Interestingly the year eighty-four corresponds to the Uranus return cycle. In this chapter I will provide several charts that help identify key and interesting life cycle points.

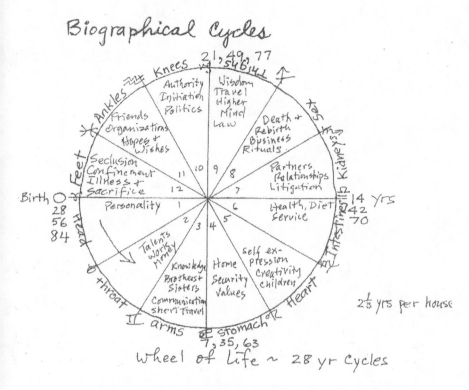

Biographical Cycles

Wheel of Life ~ 28 yr Cycles

2⅓ yrs per house

HOUSES OF THE ZODIAC AND THEIR CHARACTERISTICS

1st		2nd		3rd	
•	personality	•	talents	•	knowledge
		•	work	•	siblings
		•	money	•	communication
				•	short travel
4th		5th		6th	
•	home	•	self-expression	•	health
•	security	•	creativity	•	diet
•	values	•	children	•	service
7th		8th		9th	
•	partners	•	death and rebirth	•	wisdom
•	relationships	•	business	•	travel
•	litigation	•	rituals	•	higher mind
				•	law
10th		11th		12th	
•	authority	•	friends	•	seclusion
•	initiation	•	organization	•	confinement
•	politics	•	hopes and wishes	•	illness
				•	sacrifice

ANGULAR   SUCCEEDENT   CADENT

BODIES OF MANIFESTATION

Higher Self Ego
Sun

Man
Intellectual Soul
ego
21 years

Consciousness Soul
Spirit Self
42 years

Life Spirit
(Buddhi)
49 years

Spirit Man
(Atman)
59 years

Animals
Sentient Soul
Astral Body
14 years

Plants
Etheric Body
(Life)
7 years

Minerals
Physical Body
Birth

KEY WORDS:

PHYSICAL BODY: Mineral Kingdom, Material Substance, Law of Gravity, Centripetal Force.

ETHERIC BODY: Plant Kingdom, Life Forces, Forces of Growth in Rhythm, Centrifugal Force, Memory, Temperament.

ASTRAL BODY: Animal Kingdom, Desires, Wishes, Passions, Emotions, Feelings, Pain, Suffering, Joy.

EGO BODY: Kingdom of Man, Self Consciousness, The "I", Self Identity, Uniqueness.

In child development, birth to seven years is marked as the greatest rate of physical growth which comes to an end with the change of teeth as an indicator. During the next seven years the Etheric forces are devoted to awakening the intellectual abilities. The end of this second period is marked by the beginning of puberty and relationship consciousness. This is when the Astral Body comes to the fore with its desires, passions, likes and dislikes, emotions and feelings. In the Astrological chart we look for the Astral Body indicated in the planets and their aspects within the influences of the houses and background of the Zodiac. At twenty one the Ego comes to the fore to begin taking over personal responsibilities for one's Soul development. Prior to this the Guardian Angel acts to guide the individual. The Guardian Angel knows the destiny to be fulfilled and tries to limit harmful distractions from occurring. At thirty-five the Angel recedes into the background of responsibility and we are more on our own to triumph or regress.

SOME IMPORTANT AGES (IN YEARS)

7	Etheric body freed
9.33	self-awareness, responsibility
12	cause and effect awareness
14	Astral body freed – puberty
19	vocational decision
21	Ego body freed – adulthood
24	expansion
28	persona reborn, new beginnings
29.5	karma reveals life's work
36	build secure foundations
39	Am I doing my destiny's work?
42	psychologist's couch/relationships and career
48	vocational peak
49	time to train apprentices, let go
55	new birth of self
60	wisdom
63	personal karma is completed

INTERESTING POINTS ALONG THE WHEEL OF LIFE (AGES IN YEARS)

3 · earliest memories
 · calls self "I"

6 · lose teeth
 · start school

9 · separation from others
 · "I have a life to live."

12 · cause and effect
 · logical reasons
 · age Jesus found in
   temple

14 · puberty
 · tribal consciousness
 · gangs
 · fads
 · crushes

18.6 · philosophy
 · idealism
 · sense for future work or
   profession
 · apprenticeship/college

21 · age of majority
 · can think clearly
 · needs to go out and experience
   the world and work

26- · digest experiences since twen-
28   ty-one years old
 · isolation, loneliness or study
 · prepare for rebirth and life work

28 · rebirth
 · new personality to project
 · breaks with family
   expectations

29.5 · begin life as an individual

33.33 · connection w/destiny
 · Christ cycle

35 · expansion at work
 · family raising
 · peak of physical powers
 · Angel steps back
 · possibility for sacrifice

37.2 · expulsion
 · loss of position, friends.
 · move to new opportunities

40 · physical on wane
 · "forty years in desert,"
 · boss or administrator
 · sex, money, power
   temptations

BY BILL BRYANT AND RON ODAMA

Wheel of Life – Supplement to 28 Year Cycles
Other Important Cycles
Also Multiples and Parts

Age
(in years)

12	Jupiter ♃	• awakening • expansion • study • travel • religion • philosophy
30	Saturn ♄	• karma • tests • illness • responsibilities • fears • compulsions • duties • law cases/confinement or punishment • deaths or burdens
18.6	Moon's nodes ☊	• social awareness, connections or separations • sacrifice to groups or society
37.2	Moon's nodes ☊	• sacrifice of position or banishment
9	Moon's nodes ☊	• separation of self • life versus death • family and society • consciousness of self-responsibility

WHEEL OF LIFE – SUPPLEMENT TO 28 YEAR CYCLES
BIOGRAPHICAL TIMELINE
BASIC PLANETARY CYCLES AND NOTEWORTHY MIDPOINTS

Moon Cycles ☾	7 year periods	• rythym of individuation • self-identity/personality
Moon Nodes ☊	18.66 year periods	• rhythm of social consciousness • personal growth
Jupiter Cycles ♃	11.86 year periods	• rhythm of expansion and vocation • creativity
Saturn Cycles ♄	29.5 year periods	• rhythm of destiny and karma
Solar/ Christ Cycles ☉	33.33 year periods	• rhythm of initiation • spiritual growth

The Ego is indicated by the Sun. (See pages 27 and 32.) Of course the Ego is made up of two levels – the Personality Ego and the Higher Self, or Divine Self. In each lifetime we usually exhibit only one facet of the Higher Self.

The Moon is an indication of the Soul.

Fairy tales from The Brothers Grimm illustrate karmic development in an allegorical form, using the Prince and the King to represent the two levels of Ego. The young Soul is represented by the Princess and the older Soul is represented by the Queen and the wicked stepmother, indicating degree of redemption. If you were to create a fairy tale to illustrate a natal chart interpretation, you might find useful the additional definitions in this work's Appendix.

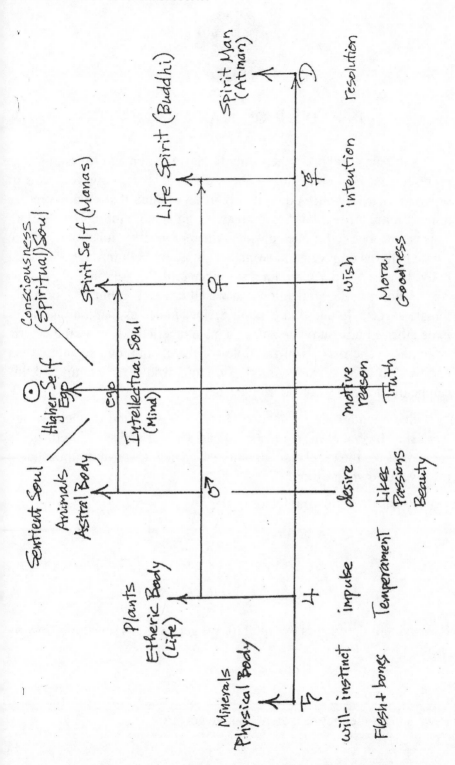

SUN AND MOON KARMIC PATTERNS

As the most important heavenly bodies, the Sun and Moon, usually represent the Ego and Soul of the individual. It is, however, hard to separate their influences definitively. I have found that man expresses himself more through his Sun sign and woman more through the Moon. This is corroborated if one considers the reproductive functions, but the cyclic patterns of seven and twenty-eight affect both through the astral body. If we consider Carl Jung's concepts of the Anima and Animus we get closer to the realization that we all have a combination of male/female aspects. In addition, Rudolf Steiner indicates that man has a female etheric body and woman has a male etheric body. And the etheric body has cyclic periods of multiples of three. Although separate, man and woman strive towards union to create a whole. An example of this can be illustrated by considering a story.

Once upon a time Pythagoras, the Greek sage and mathematician, was asked by one of his students, "What is true friendship?" Pythagoras replied, "Like the numbers 220 and 284." Then it was up to the student to solve his own question.

220 has the following factors: 1 x 220

2 x 110

4 x 55

5 x 44

10 x 22

11 x 20

If we add all the factors except 220, we get 284. 284 has the following factors: 1 x 284

2 x 142

4 x 71

If we add all the factors except 284 we get 220.

Therefore, we can conclude that 220 and 284 express the factors that make up the other. They are similar but not the same. In regards to friends or partners what one holds as the ideal for the other and helps the other to attain in life is true friendship.

Again, we must determine at what Soul level the individual is operating, to better see how the Sun and Moon are being expressed. We then can see how the male/female aspects of the self are being integrated in the individual.

THE SUN

The Sun represents the Self as divine being, as both higher Ego and lower personality ego. The process of individuation is the integration of the lower ego into a more perfect expression of the higher Ego. The prince becomes the king. The highest purpose of man's striving is to align one's self will with God's will and live accordingly. "May thy will be done, in and through me." To be able to express these perfections gives one access to infinite power. In the process we learn to express our Sun as a true individual. In the astrology chart, the sign gives a clue to the mode of expression of the spiritual archetypes through our level of consciousness. The house position tells of what department of life the integrating forces are at work. Planetary aspects between the planetary elements indicate to what degree of maturity the soul is operating through the individuality. Difficult aspects indicate challenges and harmonious aspects indicate where help is to be found usually coming from other people. The Sun shows power karma. How have we used our power? Have we used it to dominate others, or be dominated by others? The Sun must be used to show us where we must use our power to banish all shadows and must radiate purified love and light and express ourselves through joy. The Sun's position usually indicates where our life purpose can be found as our personal assignment for this incarnation. In the woman's chart the sun usually indicates those ideals held for the husband to fulfill and for the husband, those ideals he wants to express. In these days, the opposite roles can also be valid. There are many successful partnerships where the mom is working and the dad stays at home. In my life, I have seen that transits to my wife's Sun are indicators to my vocational changes.

SUN IN THE FIRST HOUSE OR ARIES

Spiritual purpose is "to be." The person strives for integration and power by discovering who they truly are and expressing their uniqueness. They must use their intelligence for leadership and apply their boundless energy. They must watch out for the tendency to dominate others and have one sided views and opinions. At the sentient soul level the person exhibits jealousy, covetousness, aggressiveness, conquest and violence. He tries to exert his selfishness. At the Intellectual soul level the person recognizes himself as an individual and learns to work with others recognizing their value. At the consciousness soul level they can act as a spiritual channel to lead community building in the service of a cause. Saint Peter is an example as he built the foundations of the Catholic Church in Rome. These people have power to lead and get things done. Another example is the football quarterback who finds a way to win, sometimes against all odds at the last second. The Aries woman is very strong and proud but seeks someone she can be proud of and look up to. This can be very difficult because her standards are high.

SUN IN THE SECOND HOUSE OR TAURUS

Spiritual purpose is "to have." This person has a desire for possessions and their stewardship. He must integrate himself by possessing material things and manipulating them in a skillful manner. This person may be challenged to develop his innate talents, including the wise use of the physical body. They have boundless energy to endure and can continue on when others are exhausted. They are excellent in sports when they develop their will because of their strength and determination to be the best. They are often found in the construction trades and in banking. They also make excellent ecologists and conservationists as they see the need to preserve the things of nature. They develop a concern for health foods and are good eaters and cooks. They must also not become hoarders out of a sense of insecurity. At the sentient soul level they find security in possessiveness. Then at the intellectual soul level they learn to use materials and talents creatively. At the consciousness soul level they rise to use resources for the good of the community. These natives must realize that resources, like talents must be used and shared and that we don't really own anything but are part of the circulation of material things. These persons must learn to look beyond the material to the spiritual. The karma of these people is to recognize their innate talents and to develop them not for themselves but for the service of others. They must not stagnate and live in the past but must let things go.

SUN IN THE THIRD HOUSE OR GEMINI

Spiritual purpose is "to know." They are endlessly seeking knowledge to improve the self. Person may be led into new knowledge, understanding and information. They are at home in the "information age." They are excellent communicators and can be found as news commentators, talk show hosts, teachers, writers and computer geeks processing information. The karma to be fulfilled is to transform the concrete mind to the spiritual mind possessing of wisdom. They must learn to make things whole, recognize patterns and find order and purpose. They must bring use of the past to integrate things of the future. At the sentient soul level the person uses the mind for personal self interest. They want to express their intelligence through argument, intellectual facts, lies and cunning. They may try to rely on dogma or rote without their own use of intelligence. At the intellectual soul level they bring knowledge to practical use and think creatively. They must break out of mind habits and express through freedom in everyday life. At the consciousness soul level the individual expresses a mental gift with pure intelligence through the arts of communication. Ideas are stimulated through environmental conditions and relationships. Public speaking and service are outlets.

SUN IN THE FOURTH HOUSE OR CANCER

Spiritual purpose is "to feel." Power is expended to establish foundations to develop the Soul. The soul becomes a concrete manifestation in the expression of the spirit. Person seeks reality with foundations of belief that can not be shaken. Person starts with examining hereditary foundations and beliefs. This is the sentient soul stage where past habits and patterns are followed dogmatically for a sense of security in the home. Food and traditions are used to insulate one from the outside world. At this stage there is always trouble with the parents, especially the father. May idolize or detest the father and he may be a victim of circumstances to which the child has no sympathy. First stage personality is vulnerable to outside influences and values and prefers to live in dreams of what could have been. Memories or influences from past lives keep intruding. In the intellectual soul level the individual gains some understanding of self and establishes goals of what he wants to become. Person wants to establish security in the home and self. At the consciousness soul level the person can express the Self with true heart consciousness with love and compassion. Spiritual foundations are established. Person realizes there is no real security in materialism. Periodic losing of home, family and possessions may be experienced to learn this.

SUN IN THE FIFTH HOUSE OR LEO

Spiritual purpose is "to radiate love." This person is moving towards self expression and release of the self as love. This includes creative self expression and children. The more Soul consciousness, the more creativity and joy can be expressed. At the sentient soul level the individual expresses his power through selfishness and ego expression at the expense of others. The prima dona at center stage. Arrogance, pride and wasting of spiritual resources are examples. Could express through a burning away of all hereditary foundations. Love for others based on projections of the self onto others or egoistic love are expressions. At the intellectual soul level there is a release of emotions with ideals expressed with concrete images through drama and artistic creations. At the consciousness soul level there is power and confidence to shape events and the environment through organizational abilities, quality of leadership and a wealth of ideas. Success comes through the earned respect and attention of the individual's magnetism or charisma. Leonardo da Vinci lived up to his name through projection of his personal power and creativity.

SUN IN THE SIXTH HOUSE OR VIRGO

Spiritual purpose is "to assimilate." This person feels creative power but can't express it and therefore experiences self consciousness and inadequacy. The will can't accomplish what the thinking desires. Therefore, there is an urge for self improvement and the need to search for deeper expressions. This leads to personal crises for growth and personal adjustments. Life centers on self centering and integration. At the sentient soul level one faces the karma of desire for power, humiliation, phobias, hypochondria and feelings of inadequacy. There can be a dogmatic attention to diet, health, nutrition and exercise. The person seeks outlets to gain confidence and seeks perfection. Often this comes through intellectual achievement. The temperament can be melancholic where there is a heightened sensitivity to pain and suffering. Virgos can be found in the helping and service professions as well as novelists and dramatists. These expressions are at the intellectual soul level. A path of devotion to an ideal or discipleship to a person are followed. At the consciousness soul level Virgos can be found devoted to causes involved with public service, health, nutrition, self improvement, unions, the military and hospitals, etc. where one can blend in with others and not be singled out. Karma is to guard against being one sided and myopic.

Sun in the seventh house or Libra

Spiritual purpose is "to relate." Pride and singleness of soul must give way to the desire for union with the other. A new world of consciousness opens as the experience of love. The individual is forced into an expansion of awareness of the needs of another. The persons' self becomes greater after they surrender the self to the other while maintaining their individuality. This also could be experienced as a union with God. On the sentient soul level the individual expresses selfishly in terms of his own needs. He can't see what others sacrifice for him and tries to control others and situations. If he does not get his way he becomes vindictive. The intellectual soul level is characterized by the need to become understanding and develop empathy for the partner. There is the recognition of the causes of loneliness and the will to do something about it. The consciousness soul stage is experienced by the possibility of blending with another or groups with compassion and love through service, cooperation and sharing with common causes. The karmic challenge is to overcome the self and blend fearlessly with others. Success brings happiness.

Sun in the eighth house or Scorpio

Spiritual purpose is "to regenerate." The personal self is to be renewed or regenerated through love. The desire is to integrate the self through creative release of emotional power. Love can mean a loss of self to blend with another. Love becomes something that is substantial, an entity of itself, created in the minds of the two people. There is a great need to join with others with love. Marriage partners pool their resources and must share everything with their partner without selfish holding back. The ego dies to build the partnership through sacrifice. "Death is the food of love." Individuals free themselves through love to become new and closer to God. The person learns to become a part of a greater whole of humanity. This is also the house of business as the individual gives up values to the business to bring about and build a stronger economy and civilization. The business acts as more than the sum of its parts – group magic. Group power is built through ceremony, rituals to conduct transactions between people and businesses. On the sentient soul level there is selfishness and an inability to truly share. Passions, selfish sex, control, domination, dishonesty and cheating, etc. are manifested. On the intellectual soul level one realizes what is required to become blended with others for a common purpose. At the consciousness soul level the Christ light can be expressed through group decision making for the benefit of the greater good of society. I have found that people with the sun in the eighth house inherit legacies from their fathers and have responsibility over the resources of others.

Sun in the ninth house or Sagittarius

Spiritual purpose is to "gain wisdom." Through self integration learned by being able to unite oneself with others brings wisdom. Knowledge is raised through experience to wisdom. We learn to go beyond the individual ego self and concreteness of facts to intuition. We are able to see patterns, think in symbols, allegories, similes, etc. to understand life. Enlightenment and compassion involves renunciation of all possessions. Every relationship that is fulfilled gives birth to understanding. Great desire to teach as a judge, teacher, priest, journalist, author, etc. Develop an intuitive sensing of essences of beauty, flowers, stones, animals, gestures, etc. of your surroundings. You need to travel and move about to expand the range of sensations. In the process one gains perspective and knows oneself better and gains universal understanding on higher spiritual levels. The Sagittarian is ready for action for he/she loves sports, travel, conversation, horses, speed, skill and excitement. On the sentient soul level the individual can be a rolling stone and never quite enter into any permanence. He/she is an incessant talker and can sell you anything including used cars. They learn not so much by reading and study but by listening. At the intellectual soul level they can become dogmatic but try to rise above it. They search for something that holds their interest and gain wisdom so they can share it. At the consciousness soul level they gain reverence for the truth and develop an unbiased clear judgment with no prejudices.

Sun in the tenth house or Capricorn

Spiritual purpose is "to achieve." They strive to realize the full potentials of power. They strive to achieve something with definite results. They bring harmony of purpose of many individuals and lead the group to fulfillment of group goals. They administer group resources responsibly or they will lose their reputation and fall from power. They may start low but keep building to rise to the top in power. They spend a lifetime striving to fulfill some kind of achievement. They can use shrewdness and planning and can be ruthless. "Ends justify the means." On the highest levels they can act as a spiritual channel. At the sentient soul level they strive to have selfish control over others and have others do what they will. They can be dishonest and cruel in achieving their goals. They love jewelry, gems and gold. Negatively they can be dictatorial and pompous with arrogance and pride. They could be blinding themselves by yearning for power they can't achieve or they may be suffering from an inferiority complex and be inhibited from taking greater responsibilities. On the intellectual soul level they recognize the importance of others and know strengths and weaknesses of others and can see how they fit into achieving group goals. They learn the right use of materiality and become great leaders. They must integrate themselves through work outside of the home in a career. At the consciousness soul level they learn to administer large groups to the benefit of all by using resources wisely. The karma is the misuse of power. Examples are the world's dictators.

Sun in the eleventh house or Aquarius

Spiritual purpose is "to serve." Individual motives are suppressed in behalf of service to the group. They must sacrifice their own welfare to the dreams and ideals of society. They can be found as members of some cause or purpose in the community such as the Chamber of Commerce, Lions, Elks, Rotary, Masons, etc. They can also be involved with ecological, ACLU, NAACP, or animal rights, etc. type of organizations. They are very conscious that they are part of the human race and must find how they may be of service. They may be without purpose until they find themselves in the right cause. They are to transform themselves to benefit society when their minds and psychic forces are integrated and group power can be focused. They will try to prove themselves as being good friends and neighbors to all people and creatures. They are upholders of culture and the arts, crusaders for the right, civilize the world through societal or scientific improvements. Bill Gates is a prime example as he tries to make internet access available to everyone. At the sentient soul level he/she will identify with friends and lose identity. They can be dogmatic and one sided in following belief systems. They may go on crusades but neglect their own family responsibilities. In relationships they never commit themselves but wish to maintain their freedom. They may intellectualize everything but never get emotionally involved. On the intellectual soul level they try to integrate themselves through involvement in groups. They learn through participation in the misuse of power. They discover which dreams and visions are founded on concrete foundations. They may rebel against conformity but have no plan of what could constructively replace the status quo. At the consciousness soul level self esteem is lost to group purpose through guidance of the spirit. They become instruments of God in the uplifting of society. They are champions of brotherhood.

SUN IN THE TWELFTH HOUSE OR PISCES

Spiritual purpose is "to understand." This is the last part of a cycle of lives and much energy is needed to learn from the past and move on into the future. Meditation is the key to make resolution. Ghosts of the past such as failures, acts of omission or commission based on selfishness must be faced by taking responsibility. All institutions of confinement such as hospitals, prisons, research laboratories, etc. may be places of work and career or confinement. One must begin to see the consequences of wrong doing. Illness may act to allow the individual to think and reflect. Welfare recipients may need time to resuscitate themselves before rejoining society to be productive again. All difficulties are caused by fears and negative attitudes. Restrictions come from inner inhibitions and complexes within the subconscious. Will and spiritual courage are to be used to overcome material bondage. These experiences bring about one's self integration when the mind and emotions are brought under control. Watch for planetary aspects for clues to the way out. Sorrow comes through negative aspects. The person needs will, courage, poise, steadiness and faith applied in service. The individual needs to become concerned for the welfare of others to lose self concern and dwelling on one's own problems. At the sentient soul level the individual must rise above past conditioning. He/she must overcome past habit patterns of thinking, feeling and willing. They must do something that they are successful at doing to gain self confidence. They are in the process of growing a soul. They can do many things well but have a tendency to not stay with things long but must be steadfast. At the same time they should not settle for routine or subordinate jobs. They must keep their spiritual light bright and resist domination. At the intellectual soul level they must become an individual and be of service. At the consciousness soul level they learn to become channels of spiritual power to act with others to bring humanitarian service projects to fruition. Since the twelfth house is the house of karma we can get a clue by the sign of the cusp as to where suffering may be coming from:

ARIES	domination by people in authority
TAURUS	occult troubles and materialism
GEMINI	sorrow through people in their close environment and relatives
CANCER	sorrow through the home life
LEO	sorrow through the opposite sex or secret love affairs
VIRGO	psychic afflictions such as obsessions, neuroses, phobias and possessions
LIBRA	painful separations in marriage
SCORPIO	powerful enemies or tragic endings
SAGITTARIUS	sorrow through persecution because of beliefs
CAPRICORN	loss of reputation through marriage and love affairs
AQUARIUS	sorrow through ill health and misuse of occult powers
PISCES	sorrow through unknown enemies

((

The Moon

The Moon represents the three levels of the soul. They have been briefly detailed in a previous chapter. The soul contains personal karmic patterns, subconscious motivations, hereditary influences, habit patterns, attitudes, unresolved emotional issues, mother and child relationships, etc. The Moon influences the personality and how one functions in the world of appearances. It is also one's other unredeemed self or double that is yet to be acknowledged and redeemed. In the man's chart the Moon describes the marriage partner and her personality, while in the woman's chart the Moon can indicate her personality and aspirations and her Sun can indicate the aspirations of her husband. The Lunation Cycle (Dane Rudhyar) can be studied to get some clues as to how the aspects between the Sun and Moon in a person's chart indicate the way the individuality expresses through the soul. On the mundane level the Moon signifies in what department of life the individual can adjust to everyday life conditions. They must remain flexible to make needed compromises to demands placed on them by others and situations by controlling their emotions.

Moon in the first house or Aries

The individual must focus on developing the persona to express his/her uniqueness in projecting the self. There may be a strong karmic tie to the mother with a need to resist bondage to expectations. In the woman's chart there may be a strong desire to mother. There may be an impulsiveness to act without due consideration. There are courage and leadership qualities also. In the man's chart Moon in Aries indicates the wife to be strong and protective of loved ones. On the sentient soul level selfishness, impulsiveness and one sidedness must be overcome. The recognition of the value of others is learned. At the intellectual soul level the intelligence is sharpened and leadership skills are developed. At the consciousness soul level the princess becomes the queen as the will is aligned to the spirit in the service of others.

Moon in the second house or Taurus

In this house the individual becomes a steward of the material goods of the earth. The individual must learn to take care of possessions including the physical body and talents. These individuals love art, music, crafts in the pursuit of beauty. They can be found in the building trades, banking and business. They love sports where strength and endurance are required. They learn by doing and develop skills. They also enjoy cooking and eating as well as farming or gardening. Since the Moon is exalted in Taurus, the emotions are very stable and under control. Relationships are lasting and committed. Moon in the second house can bring fluctuating finances where money comes and goes periodically. At the sentient soul level the passions and appetites are strong. Selfishness and possessiveness must be overcome. At the intellectual soul level skills are developed to earn money. Materialism must be overcome as one learns to be of service through work. At the consciousness soul level one learns to work with others to be successful in large enterprises such as business and manufacturing and philanthropy.

MOON IN THE THIRD HOUSE OR GEMINI

These individuals are knowledge collectors and wish to communicate information. They are very changeable with their subjective thinking. They may be given mothering responsibilities over siblings or relatives. They love to read but must learn to retain information by digging deeper to gain understanding and wisdom. They learn through conversation. They may love to be hosts at social events and are entertaining mixers. They also could be talk show hosts or news journalists or reporters. They can also make good architects and doctors but not surgeons. At the sentient soul level they can be incessant talkers and gossipers. They are filled with facts about what they have heard but lack depth of understanding. In relationships they can be Don Juans and butterflies. They may be computer geeks. At the intellectual soul level they learn to really listen to what others communicate and gain depth. They use information in practical ways and not for self gain. At the consciousness soul level they discover how their talents can be put to use for the good of humankind. They can be excellent teachers.

MOON IN THE FOURTH HOUSE OR CANCER

These individuals are very much tied to their mothers and the home and its traditions. They can be very patriotic and proud of mother, home and country. They may be very aware of their heredity and religious foundations. They may be forced to move many times like military families. They can become very emotional and teary when their feelings are aroused. They love to have family around them and celebrate festivities with traditional foods. At the sentient soul level they can be very possessive of people and possessions for security. They can be very manipulative by playing with people's emotions through expectations. At the intellectual soul level they find values that they can live with in cooperation with others with contrasting viewpoints. They learn to not equate love with control. At the consciousness soul level they become open to other people's beliefs and values and nurture people in need. They can be excellent brokers and investors in real estate.

MOON IN THE FIFTH HOUSE OR LEO

These individuals need to express their creativity with joy and enthusiasm. They can be found in the arts, music, drama, sports, education and as parents. They can use their charisma to gain popularity. They can be like the movie stars that must balance responsibilities of career and family. The ego can be too strong and they can get into trouble if they want to always get their way. They can't share the stage as equals. They can also be very noble and prideful towards their children. They can also be like the stage mother or little league coach that lives through their children's accomplishments. At the sentient soul level they exhibit selfishness through too strong of an ego. They crave adulation. At the intellectual soul level they learn to recognize the value of others. They discover their talents, develop them and recognize their limitations. At the consciousness soul level they learn to be magnanimous towards others and use their talents for the benefit of all. In the woman's chart it promises motherhood.

MOON IN THE SIXTH HOUSE OR VIRGO

Moon in the sixth house indicates the individual's need for self adjustment. There is a need to concentrate on self development, health, nutrition, diet and service to others. They can be found in the helping professions, labor unions, gymnasiums and the military. Without being of service they may have to deal with their own illness or psychological complexes and phobias. Often times they must learn to get along with coworkers. They may have a tendency to be too critical of the work of others and wish to do everything by themselves. They can become martyrs to their work and can become even more critical when pressured.

At the sentient soul level they must deal with psychological problems and self consciousness. This makes them critical of others and become loners. They may try to compensate by being intellectual. At the intellectual soul level they learn to work with others and not be too critical. They discover their talents through service. At the consciousness soul level they share what they have learned through the adjustment process, write books and be of service to help others to go through similar stages of adjustment as themselves.

MOON IN THE SEVENTH HOUSE OR LIBRA

In this house personal relationships are paramount. The individual must learn to adjust to the needs of the partner through sensitivity and empathy. This requires the ability to cooperate and compromise, putting oneself secondary to the partnership. This does not mean to become dominated and lose the individuality. This is a tendency is the Moon is in Libra and the ego wishes to be pleasant and agreeable. At the sentient soul level the selfishness must be overcome. There is a tendency to become dissatisfied with partners easily and keep seeking the perfect partner. As the perfect partner may not be seen as an individual, the person will seek a type that keeps repeating with different individuals. There may also be a wish to control the partner using psychological warfare. At the intellectual soul level the individual learns to have empathy in building relationships. The person gives up the idea of changing the partner to one's projections. At the consciousness soul level the individual learns to blend with the partner into a sound loving relationship for mutual benefit. The individual can also be a counselor to help others with relationship issues.

MOON IN THE EIGHTH HOUSE OR SCORPIO

Since the Moon is in its fall, the individual is very strong, sensuous and passionate and needs to learn control of the emotions. They may be given responsibility for the resources of others. They may be found in business, as brokers dealing in investments, or agents dealing with legacies, insurance, or estates. They have an excellent sense for the trends of business and the public's desires or new markets. They can drive hard bargains because they know the motives of others and use this to their advantage. They are very shrewd. They can ferret out obscure facts to help their case and win in court. They can salvage lost souls, failed businesses, or material goods or equipment. These individuals are interested in the occult and are like detectives in solving the mysteries of life. At the sentient soul level these individuals are ruled by their passions and emotions. They can be plagued by occult spirits or memories that intrude in dreams. At the intellectual soul level they discover their gifts and learn to put them to use without selfishness and in service. They work on getting their emotions under control. The consciousness soul level is marked by being a true steward for the resources of others. This can be in directing large business enterprises by bringing the benefit of goods and services to all. They take direction from the spiritual world.

MOON IN THE NINTH HOUSE OR SAGITTARIUS

This brings an interest in all higher mind professions and activities. This includes travel, publishing, philosophy, teaching, religion, diplomacy and metaphysics. It also may indicate a love of horses and games of chance. These individuals always seek patterns and correspondences to find meaning through experience. They are excellent in using symbolic logic to understand life's mysteries and abstract concepts. They symbolize the gaining of wisdom. They wish to communicate what they have learned. At the sentient soul level they can be incessant talkers and gamblers. They are restless and can't stay with one thing or place for long. They project a friendly and optimistic persona with many acquaintances but few friends. At the intellectual soul level they begin to focus their thinking and adapt themselves to changing conditions and people. They learn to be diplomatic and share their wisdom and knowledge. They learn to value others as individuals and not treat them as children or inferiors. An example could be Professor Henry Higgins of "My Fair Lady" who uses Eliza Doolittle in an experiment to see if language can change a flower girl into a lady to win a bet. At the consciousness soul level they use their wisdom in collegial partnership with others in large enterprises. They wish to raise the standards of culture and knowledge.

MOON IN THE TENTH HOUSE OR CAPRICORN

This brings a keen interest in political or social projects and the administration of elected mandates. It is the sign of the professional administering to the public's needs. The individual is willing to start at the bottom of large enterprises and work their way to the top. Ambition is strong to rise to power. The individual must never forget that he/she must answer to the public who put him/her in power. Scandal can topple the greatest from power with a loss of reputation. President Richard Nixon and Watergate is an example. The Moon in Capricorn person is usually considered cold and aloof and undemonstrative of love and affection. There can be a love of jewelry, precious gemstones, gold and silver. They have the capacity to judge character and to be able to build teams to work together to accomplish great projects. At the sentient soul level they must overcome selfishness and the manipulation of others for their own purposes. Ends do not justify the means. At the intellectual soul level they rise above others to use their administrative talents wisely. At the consciousness soul level they become benevolent leaders and administer well the resources of constituents. They can also rise to become initiates into spiritual consciousness.

MOON IN THE ELEVENTH HOUSE OR AQUARIUS

These individuals reflect the achievements and culture of their society. They may contribute great technological advances to the public. Women will be helpful in their endeavors. They have many friends and acquaintances but must choose them wisely. An entourage of self seekers can bleed them dry. They wish to be great humanitarians and be caught up in causes that can be impractical. They can become revolutionaries as a reflection of their desire to exert their different and independent egos. Joan d' Arc was a prototype of the nonconformist who saved France from England. She was divinely inspired to play her part in Europe's history. Moon in Aquarius people are friendly but not emotionally involved and find it difficult to fulfill relationships. They require the need to maintain their freedom, and can be cold and aloof. They can intellectualize their feelings. At the sentient soul level they are selfish and can impose on others. Their thinking is scientific, unemotional and not empathetic. Their thinking can be rigid, dogmatic and contrary. At the intellectual soul level the individual learns to become a productive member of society by using his/her intelligence and cooperating with others for the common good. At the consciousness soul level they become involved with organizations and promote service to the community and the best cultural values that society has to offer. An example are the Shriners and their hospitals for orthopedic and burn patients.

Moon in the twelfth house or Pisces

These individuals are very psychic and sensitive and otherworldly. In many ways their environment is too harsh for them to enter. It is the house of karma and there is much finishing up of previous cycles. Acts of commission and omission must be redeemed. The way to redemption is to be of service to those afflicted in hospitals and institutions without thought to personal reward or recognition. When one's personal cares are forgotten and are replaced by caring for others then karma is redeemed. One must deal with guilt and fears. Don't express pessimism around them because this can make them defeatist or passive and retreat into solitude. At the sentient soul level there can be much sorrow due to circumstances beyond their control because they are karmic returns from previous lives. They act as psychic sponges to negative influences around them. They must learn to activate their will and be constructive. At the intellectual soul level they apply their talents in service to others. They gain control of their emotions and become less affected by their environmental and psychic conditions. They can develop their musical and artistic skills to act as cathartic avenues. At the consciousness soul level they can be of great service in the relieving of the suffering of others. They can work well in hospitals, nursing homes, prisons and institutions for redemption and healing. Great beauty of soul can be developed. They learn to trust their intuitions in knowing the needs of others.

MERCURY AND VENUS KARMIC PATTERNS

☿

MERCURY

Mercury represents the mind and its use. It governs thoughts, speech, communication, writing, analysis and synthesis, memory, brain and nervous system, individual choices and selection, subjective and objective thinking. It rules two signs: Gemini and Virgo. The mind learns to gather information, communicate, to gain knowledge then learns to discriminate and judge. It is the most plastic of the planetary vibrations, having purity of emotions and neutral in gender. Mercury is the name of the Roman god and also the Greek god, Hermes. He is the god of sales, liars and thieves, for he is clever and fun loving. The house and sign indicates in what department and shading the mind can operate. The position of Mercury in relation to the Sun should be taken into account when studying the house and sign position.

Mercury's relationship to the Sun is:

- 0 to 28 degrees before (lower in degree of the same sign or previous sign) the Sun or Prometheus.

- 0 to 28 degrees after (higher in degree of the same sign or latter sign) the Sun or Epimetheus.

Mercury can either be direct or retrograde.

There are four cases that can be considered for interpretation:

1. PROMETHEUS DIRECT – Mercury rising before the Sun crossing the ascendant clockwise first. This indicates a strong focalized mental activity that rebels against bodily desires and instincts. The mind takes control of irrational urges of the astral body. It also rebels against religious and cultural traditions. The mind desires to develop a clear,

rational mind to determine one's individuality and life purpose. The Virgo qualities are needed to counteract Gemini's enthusiasm for acquiring facts and getting lost in superficialities.

2. PROMETHEUS RETROGRADE – These individuals experience an initiation into the inner side of being. Trust or interest is lost of the ordinary impulses of the nature. They know they must leave the instinctual impulses behind. The person identifies with causes or struggles of the outer world knowing that inner conflict produces growth on mental levels.

3. EPIMETHEUS DIRECT – Mercury rising after the Sun indicates a conservative mind looking to the past with historical perspective. They learn from events that have happened. The mind is deliberate, evolutionary, building on experience, scientific, associative, recapitulative, generalizing and analyzing. The mind is slowing down and becoming more deliberate and calm. There is a practical orientation in dealing with people and situations. They can be formal and materialistic in their approach in their approach to life and relationships.

4. EPIMETHEUS RETROGRADE – The person is developing inwardly toward self integration. They deliberately seek God and their own origin. They use knowledge to seek inner guidance. The mind is metaphysical, religious and philosophical. They study history and traditions but will not become dogmatic.

Some problems with Mercury retrograde are that the conscious control of the mind is loosened. They have trouble in making their thoughts clear to people around them. Their self expression is blocked but their minds are clear. They can withdraw into a mental world of their own. They may have difficulty in controlling their psychic energy. The mind can be operating more profoundly while changing to become more intuitive. They may have bouts of forgetfulness, have loss of memory on a selective basis and become thoughtless.

Karmically, their subconscious patterns are being worked on. They seem to always be preoccupied with something within. They are working on strong mental complexes from past incarnations. The mind can be temporarily suspended in the subconscious while sorting out thoughts coming from memories. They are learning to think in terms of symbols, patterns and abstracts through intuition. Subtlety of the mind is being evolved.

Mercury in the first house or Aries

These individuals are quick witted, intelligent, impatient, impulsive and argumentative. They are quick to take action and like to test their wits against others in argument. They are men and women of action. They can size up situations very quickly. They must learn to control the will and consider consequences of speech and deed.

Mercury in the second house or Taurus

These individuals are conservative and materialistic in thought. They learn by doing and developing skills. They can be artistic or musically inclined. They can be stubborn in thought and acquisitive of material goods for security. They may be good in business, construction, trades, banking, assembly and office work. They can be thorough but plodding.

Mercury in the third house or Gemini

These people are focused on information and communication and can be very successful in working with computers and the internet. They have very sharp minds and need constant change and challenges. They can be avid readers and communicators working as writers, journalists, news reporters and commentators.

Mercury in the fourth house or Cancer

These individuals are concerned about traditional home or family values. They may move around seeking security and stability. They are very emotional and subjective in thinking. They may be interested in geneology and history. They may be very successful in dealing in real estate, cooking or baking. They invest themselves in their creations, including children. They can be very possessive. They may like to collect antiques or become docents in a museum.

Mercury in the fifth house or Leo

These individuals can use their mind creatively and can project their ideas through speech and drama. They may write love novels or children's stories. They must learn to not be opinionated and rigid. They can also be very proud and dictatorial. They may love sports and gambling.

MERCURY IN THE SIXTH HOUSE OR VIRGO

These individuals are very analytical, interested in health and diet and can become too self concerned. Their minds can be hard to control as they have a tendency to think too much. They can be planning and considering all options when thinking about possible outcomes or scenarios of events. This can lead to worrying about events that never happen. "Paralysis by analysis." This may lead to nervousness and health problems. A possible avenue is to be of service in the health fields and rehabilitation programs. They lose interest when patients or clients do not respond to self development.

MERCURY IN THE SEVENTH HOUSE OR LIBRA

These individuals are focused on relationships. They may marry someone younger than themselves. The mind can be vacillating and indecisive when making decisions. They may be perfectionists and critical when esthetics are a factor. They make good attorneys and can argue cases or peruse documents in detail. They have a very positive mind but may appear calm and pleasant in personality.

MERCURY IN THE EIGHTH HOUSE OR SCORPIO

Mercury here can bring legacies from the dead or money from the partner. They must learn to manage the resources of others wisely. They must be careful with legal contracts and agreements. They may deal with wills, estates, insurance, etc. or be involved with salvaging the proceeds of businesses.

MERCURY IN THE NINTH HOUSE OR SAGITTARIUS

Mercury expands the mind's horizons and has interest in philosophy, foreign lands, higher education, publishing, law and diplomacy. It also rules in-laws. The mind must learn to be down to earth and practical. Theories, abstracts and generalities become boring and useless without application.

MERCURY IN THE TENTH HOUSE OR CAPRICORN

Mercury in this house and sign brings steadiness and practicality. The individuality will have the ability to plan and administer group efforts in large projects. It gives the ability to speak and communicate to build team efforts. Public relations and reputation are important. They are apt to become too serious and lacking in empathy. They need to meditate and develop a connection to the spirit.

MERCURY IN THE ELEVENTH HOUSE OR AQUARIUS

These individuals are focused on friends, groups and organizations. They are involved with humanitarian causes. Their minds are sharp, creative and scientific. They are in their element using technology and computers. The mind can be restless and not concentrative as well as rigid. They are excellent speakers and writers.

MERCURY IN THE TWELFTH HOUSE OR PISCES

In this house and sign the individuals are dreamy, psychic and instinctual. The mind needs to be harnessed and more practical. It is hard to see the forest, for the trees. Confusion brings passivity as if they are always in a fog. There are many fears arising from the subconscious and unconscious. They feel that they have failed to finish things and say their will is weak. They are seeking an avenue to be of service.

♀

VENUS

Venus is the planet of love and relationships. Its position tells where and how our desire for personal relationships and sharing of values will meet us through people.

Venus was the goddess that was born from the sea's depths. She is beautiful, attractive and pure in intentions. She represents the highest ideals of love. However, she can easily be led astray by selfishness and the lower passions. Venus also has to do with business and commerce and the flow of money and resources. There can be no hoarding. Venus has to do with music and the arts and the striving for the divine in its expressions. Venus rules two signs: Taurus and Libra. The Taurean Venus indicates how one values possessions, labor, arts and music. The Libran Venus indicates how one values relationships, social and aesthetic interests.

Like Mercury we study Venus in its relation to the Sun. This indicates a person's individual emotional temperament and how he/she relates to situations and people. Venus in relationship to the Sun is:

- 0 to 47 degrees before (lower in degree of Lucifer same sign or in previous sign).

- 0 to 47 degrees after (higher in degree of Hesperus same sign or in later sign)

Venus can also be direct or retrograde. Venus retrograde happens for six weeks out of every 584 days, so it is rare. Venus retrograde indicates an ascetic personality that values in a more personal sense, which contradicts instinctual reactions to life's experiences. Artistic and musical expressions are idiosyncratic in nature.

There are two cases that we will consider for interpretation:

1. VENUS LUCIFER – Seen in the morning sky rising before the Sun. This indicates a more spontaneous human responsiveness to situations and relationships. This rushing into experience may cause disappointments when creating unexpected or negative responses. This then may cause sensitivity against showing emotions or affections. It also indicates a high sense of values which are projected into life's experiences of the self and others. The individual uses their emotions and intuitions as their guide.

2. VENUS HESPERUS – Seen in the evening sky after sunset. This person judges actions by the effects that are produced in a historical perspective. Emotional responses can be intense but not as spontaneous. He/she does not allow the emotions to direct his/her daily life but will exert more judgment to emotional responses. There can be selfless devotion to religious traditions. There can also be a lack of personal warmth or expressions.

VENUS IN THE FIRST HOUSE OR ARIES

These individuals are usually charming and attractive in personality. They wish to integrate what love experiences and cultural influences bring to them. They can be very musical or artistic.

VENUS IN THE SECOND HOUSE OR TAURUS

This usually brings talents, money and harmony to the body's movements. The person is attractive to money and resources. They love to create beauty, cook, eat and work with plants and gardens. They can be good workers with the earth's products. Many work in construction or the skilled trades. They must be careful not to value materialism too strongly.

VENUS IN THE THIRD HOUSE OR GEMINI

These individuals bring warmth to relatives, neighbors and others in their everyday environment. They love to exchange pleasantries with their communications. They can write poetry, verses and songs. They may have cared for brothers or sisters or visa versa. They make good receptionists or hosts as they can make strangers feel comfortable.

VENUS IN THE FOURTH HOUSE OR CANCER

To this person home and family traditions and relations are important. Their home is their castle and they feel the most comfortable at home. They are very much concerned with their home life and want it to be beautiful and pleasant as a representation of themselves. They can be very tenacious to hold or defend what is theirs. They usually have a pleasant end of life.

VENUS IN THE FIFTH HOUSE OR LEO

These people must express their ego through their creative talents. They gain much enjoyment through children, art, music, drama, jewelry, sports, etc. Love affairs bring happiness when their projections are reflected in another. They are noble and proud and have charisma.

VENUS IN THE SIXTH HOUSE OR VIRGO

These individuals are usually blessed with good health and when ill they receive loving care. They love to give service and help to others. They have good relations with coworkers. They are very self conscious and always working on self improvement. They work best with women. This position can give Venus a too mental aspect to love and affection, resulting in less spontaneity. They have too much consideration of health, cleanliness and hygiene.

VENUS IN THE SEVENTH HOUSE OR LIBRA

Venus in this house and sign brings benefits in relationships. Good karma built in the past brings harmony and gain through people one encounters in life. People are ready to help when in times of need. Contracts and partnerships are favored.

VENUS IN THE EIGHTH HOUSE OR SCORPIO

All products of partnerships are favored. One usually gains through marriage, legacies, business, affairs of the dead, insurance etc. Women bring favorable advantage in contracts and agreements. This position also favors investments with uncanny right timing.

VENUS IN THE NINTH HOUSE OR SAGITTARIUS

These individuals are always shooting for far distant horizons to widen their wisdom. They may travel and live in foreign lands or marry someone born in another country. They are attracted to the unfamiliar and are restless in pursuit of the new. They have an interest in religion, philosophy, law, diplomacy, languages, higher education, publishing, writing, etc.

VENUS IN THE TENTH HOUSE OR CAPRICORN

These individuals are favored in their professions. They may gain position through the influence of women. Their mothers may have had a big influence in their guidance toward their profession. Honors, favors and position are received through hard work and attention to the needs of the many in their care. This also favors artistic and musical vocations.

VENUS IN THE ELEVENTH HOUSE OR AQUARIUS

This position brings benefits through friends and associations. Much good works can be accomplished in society through humanitarian projects benefiting the common person. There can be a knack in using technology to broadcast one's communications. There is the ability to attract money and resources to worthy causes. Bill Gates and Paul Allen are good examples of the intentions of this house and sign. Cultural activities are favored.

VENUS IN THE TWELFTH HOUSE OR PISCES

These individuals are concerned with completing personal or societal cycles. They wish to move forward with the best that is due. They may feel alone but there is always someone there to help in times of need. Care can be given or received in giving service to those with disabilities, illness, incarceration, rehabilitation, etc. There is little regard for material rewards. But like Cinderella, she can rise up out of the ashes to become the queen through beauty of soul.

MARS AND JUPITER KARMIC PATTERNS

♂

MARS

Mars is the opposite of Venus. Whereas Venus receives, Mars acts. It is the planet of will. Where it is placed by house and sign it indicates where one discovers the self through interaction with one's environment. The will needs to develop courage, enterprise, strength, initiative and perseverance. Challenges will arise to test the self. The use of will projects us into future lives. After life we are judged by what we have done with our speech and actions. Much of the will is hidden in our unconscious as we continually try to bring more consciousness to it. We do not know what makes our hand move. Sometimes we have not thought about it. Musical instruments cannot be played when we think too much. In sports, practice makes perfect. We try to reach the point of non-thinking and we are in "the zone." We react. The karma of Mars is the wrong use of the will. Life then brings challenges to learn the right use of will and to make amends. At the sentient soul level we react negatively or act in selfishness. It manifests as hasty actions, accidents, recklessness or carelessness. On the mental level it can act as excessive activity, talking or thinking or planning. At the intellectual soul level we learn cause and effect. Mars must learn to be balanced, and use caution in the use of will and to learn patience. The individual develops moral action, perseverance and concentration. And at the consciousness soul level we learn to use our will in service to the greater good. Mars must learn to be well directed to accomplish worthy purposes of the will. When Mars is weak by sign, aspects or placement it shows weakness in focusing the will. In the male chart this can be a lack of initiative and follow-through. In the female this can also be true but a danger can be to become overly aggressive.

Mars rules Aries and Scorpio. In Aries there is strength of personality projection and in Scorpio the motives and emotions gain strength. Mars in a house reveals the field of experience in which energy and initiative can most successfully be applied. Mars can be direct or retrograde. When it is direct force is directed outwardly into life. When Mars is retrograde, it is placed in opposition to the Sun, and force is directed inwardly to transform the ego and astral body. The personality is being transformed.

Mars in the First House or Aries

Mars in this house and sign brings strength to the projection of the persona. It has the power to scorch and burn or to heal and encourage others. These people make good leaders, debaters, initiators or organizers. They have talent to think fast, make decisions administer and are self sufficient, and self reliant. On the highest levels they can be very intelligent and make great humanitarians.

Mars in the Second House or Taurus

These people can be excellent at working with things of the earth. They can handle money, tools, the earth, metals and banking/investment instruments. They have strong appetites, stamina, athleticism, and dexterity. They can develop their talents and skills to express themselves through hard work and dedication. Music and art can be good outlets. A green thumb can show when they work with plants.

Mars in the Third House or Gemini

Mars here can focus the will in communication of ideas through writing, speaking, the internet, teaching, etc. They are forever gathering information and conveying it to others. They must learn to gain depth of insight and be less superficial. They make good reporters but not necessarily good leaders. They like to follow, are fashion conscious, and like to make impressions. They love uniforms.

Mars in the Fourth House or Cancer

They want to establish home, security, family traditions, patriotism, and dynasties. This position would be good for officers in the military, especially the Navy. They must learn to control the emotions and not be so reactive when the status quo is challenged. They may defend their beliefs blindly. They may use cooking to gain affection.

MARS IN THE FIFTH HOUSE OR LEO

These individuals need to express their creativity through self projection. They love children, dramatic arts, music, and all creative expressions. They may have charisma and rule by divine right. Their challenge is to temper their pride and selfishness.

MARS IN THE SIXTH HOUSE OR VIRGO

The will is usually focused on self improvement. They can be critical, perfectionists, health nuts, vegetarians, hypochondriacs or have psychological complexes. Their will has been blunted so they turn inwardly to gain confidence by being successful. Intellectualism may be their crutch. They need to find ways to be of service to counteract too much self concern.

MARS IN THE SEVENTH HOUSE OR LIBRA

These individuals seek to find fulfillment through building lasting relationships. They have many partners of all kinds to discover the self through cooperation, harmony, and sharing. Since they can see all sides of every issue, they make good contract attorneys, brokers, mediators, arbitrators, and diplomats. There may be strife in partnerships until selfishness is overcome.

MARS IN THE EIGHTH HOUSE OR SCORPIO

In this house and sign the will is directed to evaluate the fruits of relationships. There can be no superficial relationships. All motives and problems of relationships will be probed. They ask, "What is your commitment?" They will wish to manage investments, legacies, regenerate businesses, salvage proceeds, process insurance claims, negotiate contracts, investigate other planes of existence, dreams, etc. Their karma is to learn to control anger, passions and manage their emotions. This can also be an indicator of violence or violent death.

Mars in the ninth house or Sagittarius

In this house and sign the will is directed to expand the mind in the search for wisdom. This Mars reaches for far horizons both physically and mentally. A universal philosophy is being developed to include all streams of beliefs. They would make excellent professors or clergy as well as anthropologists, philosophers, linguists, judges, and diplomats. The danger here is to become an "ivory tower" expert with no practical grounding.

Mars in the tenth house or Capricorn

These individuals strive to be the top of their profession. They have patience to work hard and rise by steps through sheer persistence toward their goals. Like the billy goat they seek the highest point in the barnyard. They strive to be the esteemed leader with an immaculate reputation. They make excellent CEOs of large corporations or the government.

Mars in the eleventh house or Aquarius

The will is directed towards building associations with others of like minded purposes. Friends are very important in the pursuit of common goals or causes. Associations are built for the common good. There can be very high humanitarian goals such as community service, marshalling money for hospitals, etc.

Mars in the twelfth house or Pisces

The will is directed to learn from the past and to move on into a new cycle. If there is much karma to clear, there can be much suffering, violence or isolation. One may need time out of the mainstream of life to meditate and contemplate. There may be a history of drugs and alcohol addiction. Illness may play a role here, as well as demonic possession. The soul may need catharsis which can be relieved through art and music. Later, these persons can get reoriented towards the positive by being of service to those who are limited and suffering in prisons, institutions, hospitals, etc. One unusual case of how this can be worked out is of a man who was a court reporter who had to record the results of serious crimes on a daily basis.

24

JUPITER

Jupiter is the planet of socialization. It gives the impulse to expand beyond ourselves. Through Jupiter we experience faith, trust, optimism, expansion, philosophy, wisdom, spirituality, justice in law, initiation, publishing, teaching, distant travel, sports/games, horses and gambling. It rules the signs Sagittarius and Pisces. Its symbol is the Centaur, as Chiron was the teacher of Aristotle and other heroes. Benevolence is related to Pisces, understanding and the feet. Sagittarius is related to the eyes, thighs and sciatic nerves, and movement forward. Jupiter rules the liver, which is the largest organ of life as it stores glucose and energy of the body as it helps to purify the blood. It is also related to the metal tin. The ego is strongly attached to the liver, as it needs warmth and energy to do work. Jupiter has to do with the striving of the ego to unite with the Higher Ego. Experience is the teacher as the astral body is purified in the pursuit of wisdom. This requires recognition of patterns, allegories, synchronicity, in the events of the life. Knowledge gained from experience is transformed into wisdom. Scientific methodology and hypothesis testing are based upon Jupiterian thinking. Experiments are designed to test hypothesis. One can't believe in the truth of results unless it is experienced using probabilities. One must develop faith to proceed and grace can't work in life without openness and faith. "Is this all luck or is it fate?" "Do we have free will, or is everything fated?" These are the types of questions that Jupiter asks.

When Jupiter is weak by sign, aspects or placement it shows negative ego expressions. The ego can be expressed both positively or negatively. It can be expressed as over optimism, bombastic behaviors, over expansion, going beyond reasonable bounds, exaggeration, reliance on dogma or charisma, lying and deceit. Contrarily, it can be expressed as lack of confidence or faith, pessimism, scattered thinking, inconsequential chatter and talk, lack of intelligence, narrow mindedness, lack of planning and untruthfulness. In group work there can be a lack of faith in each other, lack of group decisions, reliance on dogma and process, lack of spiritual direction and decisions based upon pragmatism. Then the consciousness soul can't enter into manifestation. A good working of Jupiter can bring good heartedness, faith and optimism, broad mindedness, expansive benevolence and reliance in the spirit.

A retrograde Jupiter indicates lessons to be learned in the proper use of the ego. One must overcome hardship to gain faith and optimism in the self. Then one can become a tower of strength as an example to others. The house indicates the sector of life where these challenges can be of focus. An example is the life of Franklin D. Roosevelt in which he overcame the effects of polio to rise to the presidency.

Jupiter in the first house or Aries

Jupiter here brings a persona that projects largeness, magnanimity, optimism, expansiveness, and good heartedness. They can make good leaders and administrators. They rise to these positions through merit and strength of personality. The danger is to rely too much on the ego and over expand.

Jupiter in the second house or Taurus

Material interests provide the vehicle to project the ego. These individuals have big plans and dreams for their business interests. They like money and possessions and pursue the good life. Like Diamond Jim Brady they may overeat and feed their passions. Fortunes can be gained and lost due to overexpansion.

Jupiter in the third house or Gemini

This person makes an excellent teacher and communicator. They have a "You can do it!" personality. They are forever learning and gathering facts to communicate. The internet is a good outlet for their interests. The danger here is in not being grounded in their ideas: they may lack practicality.

Jupiter in the fourth house or Cancer

These individuals project the ego in building home, family traditions, security, belief systems, and lavish surroundings. They usually have inherited much and have many choices in pursuits. The end of life is usually comfortable with good care. Their task is the pursuit of truth. They usually don't travel long distances unless they take their homes with them – recreational vehicle, yacht, etc.

JUPITER IN THE FIFTH HOUSE OR LEO

These people project the ego to receive adulation for their charisma and talents. They gain enjoyment through children, fun and games, gambling, sports and love affairs. They attract gifts and attention. They can be movie stars and celebrities using native beauty or talents. The danger is to become big headed and lose perspective while attracting similar personalities.

JUPITER IN THE SIXTH HOUSE OF VIRGO

This is not a good position for Jupiter for it can become too myopic in perspective. Jupiter can't express itself freely because there is too much mind/analysis. This is an attempt to control life's situations. If things do not go their way then they become too critical and make the lives of others miserable. "Paralysis through analysis" is the saying that describes this. Jupiter can be useful through self development and service to others. Operating a health spa, gymnasium or nutrition store, or becoming a natural healing practitioner are examples of good outlets. Care needs to be taken when dealing with co-workers or employees because indiscretions can't be allowed to pass without consequences.

JUPITER IN THE SEVENTH HOUSE OR LIBRA

Here, Jupiter usually brings gain through partnerships. The partner must be allowed to shine as one's own ego takes a back seat but gains through vicarious experiences. These individuals build partnerships with many people as reflections of different aspects of the self. An example of this is to listen to teenage girls talk about what they like about their friends' behaviors. In Rudolf Steiner's view we alternate lives as male and female to move towards wholeness.

JUPITER IN THE EIGHTH HOUSE OR SCORPIO

These individuals gain from the fruits of relationships. There is gain from legacies, estates, and inheritances. There is a knack in managing other people's money and investing wisely. These people can be very shrewd, evaluating motives and negotiating agreements to their benefit. There is also the aspect of salvaging failures and resurrecting them to be greater than before. Dreams and the spiritual world are of interest and can bring benefits. In relationships, the possibility of blending with another exists. Rituals and protocol are used with power to build relationships toward common purposes.

Jupiter in the ninth house or Sagittarius

This is an excellent placement for Jupiter, as there is always expansion of consciousness to be all inclusive. The mind is searching for wisdom, aligning one's will with the Christ's will to be of greater service. These individuals can relate to people of all strata of society as they strive to be universal citizens. Their higher educational goals are always favored. They can become leaders in all Sagittarian endeavors.

Jupiter in the tenth house or Capricorn

This placement indicates professional outlets for the ego. These natives rise to executive positions based upon merit and leadership qualities. This is a good placement for CEOs, bishops, cardinals and popes. They benefit from powerful people to rise to power. It can also be an indication of striving for initiation into higher consciousness.

Jupiter in the eleventh house or Aquarius

This position brings challenges to the ego to lead in community service for the benefit of all. Friends and associations are important to further personal aims and projects. Very large undertakings can be led and become successful. Technology can be used to benefit society. They can be very successful as computer programmers, scientists, and engineers, etc. They can also promote culture and the very best that society has to offer.

Jupiter in the twelfth house or Pisces

These individuals are directed to complete a cycle of lives by redeeming sins of commission and omission. They can rely on help from the spiritual world through communication with their Angels. There is last second help in times of need. The ego is expressed best through selfless service with compassion and love. They can rescue lost souls by sharing what they themselves have gained through experience and contemplation. These individuals need solitude for meditation, reflection and prayer. They can penetrate into the unconscious and subconscious.

SATURN KARMIC PATTERNS

♄

Saturn is the planet of karma. Saturn represents form and restrictions. One feels the greatest vulnerability – lack, handicaps, obstructions, crosses to bear. Saturn pinpoints your Achilles' heel. Prayers for relief are not answered because you need the experience. Resigning yourself to "thy will be done" will bring transformational results on inner development.

Saturn represents the instinct of self preservation and development of identity. The house position tells the area of vulnerability to embarrassment and hurt, but also our potential greatest strength. We must use planning, patience, perseverance, hard work, honesty and practicality to gain success. It is our crown of thorns to gain inner security and face fears. We must grapple with fears and transform them to grow to maturity, Saturn indicates the security urge and tests of inertia and resistance to change. We must develop inner security – "Let go and let God."

Negative Saturn expressions would be to deny one's own responsibilities, snobbishness, running others down, being a hypocrite, or living on other people's work as a parasite. This would also include allowing extreme melancholic tendencies to gain power, such as using illness or handicaps to gain control of others to be your servants. Negative Saturn expressions also include self-mortification and denial of the body and its needs such as self-flagellation, anorexia, "measuring your way to Jerusalem," as well as disregarding the body as a physical form of the spirit.

On the mental level, Saturn expresses itself as dogma, prejudice, mental tyranny, closed mindedness, opinionated/rigid views, duty, idiocy, etc. Guilt and remorse complexes are also shown by Saturn. Redeem through belief, spirit, and its goodness. One must become open minded and a true seeker of the truth. Strive to be conscious of joyous fulfillment of responsibilities, and to be a servant for the good, beautiful, and true. Unite Mars energies with Saturn by being more benevolent. Additionally, by uniting Jupiter with Saturn, we gain faith and optimism to overcome fears. In using Neptune energies with Saturn, healing and connection to the spiritual hierarchies – music, art, mathematics, psychic abilities – is brought about. Uranus energies with Saturn will break down crystallizations, dogma, etc. Pluto united with Saturn can bring psychological healing of ancient karma from the soul depths of the unconscious and has the potential power to transform all of humankind. Moon in harmony with Saturn brings benevolent, tender feelings of love, nurturing, protective, mothering care.

In short, Saturn is the planet of alchemy to transmute all karma into initiation of the individual to the spirit – "Gold from base metals." Patience, the right use of time, cyclic plus linearity produces spirals into the future, practicality/reality, utility, perseverance, responsibility, clarity, etc., are the ways of Saturn. Other planets in aspect to Saturn must serve Saturn first before they are free to express their own natures. A retrograde Saturn turns energy inward to work on the ego. In regards to karma, it indicates immaturity in the use of Saturn's properties. When there are no negative aspects to Saturn it indicates maturity and can bring patience and help to other planets. Trines to Saturn show great maturity in the working of both planets.

SATURN IN THE FIRST HOUSE OR ARIES

These individuals are building a personality to reflect the ego. They take life seriously and start out shy, self conscious, timid and nervous to take up challenges. They expect the worst and want to be ready for it. They must develop the personality to overcome fear of new situations. They can't let anyone but the self be responsible for their own security. They can be critical, practical, skeptical and wish to evaluate through their own experiences and not by what others say. Saturn teaches not to accept defeat but to overcome hardships. They must fulfill themselves as an individual as they may not have done this in the past lives. So, fate manifests early in life to teach strength of character. They must overcome anxiety, feelings of inferiority, and fear. They develop a sense of dignity and worth and can't accept anything less than perfection. They can be like a general plotting his campaigns. If Saturn's commandments are followed, they develop prudence, practicality, patience, common sense, and right use of time. Then, after the first twenty-eight years they gain more ease and freedom. They can become good leaders. They can have a very difficult birth and experience illness and weakness in the early years.

Saturn in the Second House or Taurus

These individuals develop right attitudes toward materiality. Money and resources are important to them as they are related to their sense of security. They need to have the ability to pay on demand and would be humiliated if they have to depend on others in money matters. They concentrate their efforts on getting or making money. They may need to be known to others to have this money security. They can be thrifty and good money managers. They are price conscious and want to get full value for their money. They may have to work hard to spend money and will feel poor no matter how much money they have. They could hang onto their job rather than risk their security. They could become bitter or hateful towards others who they think have more. Saturn here may bring responsibilities to develop talents or the right use of the body to develop skills. Income may be limited until right attitudes toward money are developed.

Saturn in the Third House or Gemini

These individuals are developing the right use of thinking and com-munication. Saturn acts as a brake to excessive use of the mind, speech and activity. One can read many books but not know what was read. Excessive talk or computer use may be indications of the wrong use of the mind. They can be sticklers for details and can be discreet and formal in relationships with people in their environment. They dislike routine and can be reticent about their own affairs. They can be sensitive about other people's reactions in every day interactions and need to become better communicators. They may have a speech defect or dyslexia. They may also have no brothers or sisters or have had to take care of them at a young age. They may have been deprived of normal family patterns and are not at ease with peers. They must watch out to not develop rigid habit patterns that rule the life or excessive repetitive behaviors or thoughts. They may talk prematurely about their plans that diminish their strength. They could make excellent reporters of the news.

SATURN IN THE FOURTH HOUSE OR CANCER

These people are building unshakable foundations of their security. They want to make their home and family as their refuge. They guard their privacy. They hang onto family traditions, beliefs, and inheritances. They can be the patriarchal type in establishing a family line. They need to switch to security based upon inner spiritual foundations. They can be possessive and want to control through the use of food and obligations. They don't want to be dependent on anyone for their security. Discipline is built into them and don't want their authority defied. They may become dictatorial to keep their family solidarity intact. They are good providers but are not lavish or pretentious in choice of home. Pride makes them good hosts but may be very discriminating, choosy, or practical about who is invited into the home.

SATURN IN THE FIFTH HOUSE OR LEO

All personal motivations are centered in the need to express themselves without restrictions. They like to rule and resent anyone in authority over them. They insist on the choosing of their own destiny. These people are usually loyal, reliable, and simple in character. It is necessary to express their creativity and responsibility through their children in this life. They have great patience in their care. They may have difficulty in expressing their love and are inhibited sexually. Children with this placement should be treated with gentleness and encouraged to express themselves through arts, sports, drama, and music and learn to lose and take constructive criticism without feeling hurt. It is difficult to find happiness in romance but they are totally committed when it gets going.

SATURN IN THE SIXTH HOUSE OR VIRGO

These individuals focus their personal motivations on work, self improvement and adjusting to society. This position brings great depth to work or suffering. They may rebel against any social or economic duty. They may get sick to avoid going to social functions. They give great attention to accuracy by being serious and thorough. They have a sense of responsibility to self improvement and to one's work. They may express

"All work and no play." They may develop a nagging nature, are pedantic, or desire to work alone. They learn to break out of negative thought patterns. Negative thinking can bring on health problems. Hypochondria may result. They must develop prudence and self discipline and the ability to work with coworkers. They may be such perfectionists that no one can do the work well enough to suit them and they try to do everything themselves. Therefore, anxiety and insecurity exist in work, service, and health. These individuals can become excellent at organizing any task to move smoothly to completion through teamwork.

SATURN IN THE SEVENTH HOUSE OR LIBRA

The emphasis here is to be able to develop healthy relationships with partners. They must learn to give and take and to learn to cooperate in harmony. There is a need to relate with empathy. Saturn here may be an indication of being a loner in past lives. They must learn to retain individuality while learning to blend with another. There can be no dominance without freedom for both. These people may be very cautious in reaching out to others and may be very careful or cautious about marriage or partnerships. They can be disliked because their feelings don't flow out well and they are misunderstood. Karmic fulfillment is through marriage. Marriage may be a negative experience if Saturn is negatively aspected. They must learn to make sacrifices, compromises, and cooperate. They will be vulnerable to people who are inconsiderate and selfish until they learn self confidence to demand equality. Otherwise they could be martyrs, give all and be rejected. They may have trouble finding a partner meeting their specifications because if they can't accept themselves, they can't accept others either. There is a fear to love because there is a fear of rejection. They may marry older partners seeking material security or a parent figure. They may also marry someone who has disabilities or handicaps. They may have long term partners that never culminate in marriage. After trials and tribulations can become excellent negotiators or marriage counselors.

SATURN IN THE EIGHTH HOUSE OR SCORPIO

All personal motivations are centered on adjusting to social expectations and pressures. They are sensitive to family, group and national expectations. They adjust their inner self to their outer lot in life. This can bring depth to self ordering, self discipline, and reorientation to order.

By doing this they give example by poise. They have an intense, serious attitude. They can make great researchers and metaphysicians because they are resourceful, persistent and skilled. They can become an adept or initiate through deep occult investigations. They contact other planes of consciousness. They develop good insight into motives and values and can be of help to solve psychological problems. Saturn here may experience heart break or loss of loved ones to see beyond the material to the spiritual. They can also regenerate situations and like the phoenix rise from the ashes of defeat. They reorient themselves and start new patterns and build with better standards. They can be blunt and "call a spade a spade." They hate to be politically correct and not see the truth. They have the ability to handle other people's money and resources if not afflicted. If afflicted by aspects they tend to be melancholic and depressed as they have difficulty in letting go of things that have lost their usefulness. They may hang onto materialistic values and can't appreciate intangible or spiritual values. They have the danger of being too passive and wait for things to come to them. This causes the results of missed opportunities. Saturn also brings legacies from the father.

SATURN IN THE NINTH HOUSE OR SAGITTARIUS

All personal motivations are centered on the intellectual level or by vicarious experience. They are very sensitive to competency of other people's judgment. They make them cite their expertise before believing them. They are very sure of their own judgment as competent. In past lives they may have been too gullible or dishonest. In this life they have a strong sense for justice and the truth. They have a deep interest in philosophy and wisdom. They may have legal talent and what they say may be taken seriously. They may have a whimsical sense of humor disguising a profound philosophical mystique. They may use nonsensical expressions to parody the truth. An example during the civil rights movement was "Would you want your sister to marry a real estate broker?" The mind is reflective, contemplative and meditative. This makes them critical and demanding in regards to religion or organized society. Their philosophy tends toward a pragmatic worldly outlook that can have a sophisticated tolerance. Poet, philosopher, judge, or teachers are good professions for them. They do extensive reading, travel and study. They are secure in the present because they can draw from experiences in past lives. A danger is to try to live in the past where they felt more comfortable or in a world that might have been. They should instead take the best of the past and build upon it.

SATURN IN THE TENTH HOUSE OR CAPRICORN

All personal motivations center on group experience, matters of authority, individual prominence, or prestige. They are focused on one's place in the world. They are sensitive to political or business power or position. They have good diplomatic abilities or economic sense. They move slowly and surely towards success, are patient, concentrative, and have self restraint to not overreact in situations that arise. They may have good diplomatic abilities or an economic sense. They must learn that their foundations of power must be firm and stable and they must not do anything to lose reputation or they will fall. They can't climb to the top without the support of the group and must take responsibility for the group. Their karma is that they look for security from someone above them in authority. It is first their parent, then another authority figure. They must learn to become dependent on themselves and not on an authority figure. Too much self judging must become self reverence, self knowledge, and self control. These virtues raise men to power, as they will face every kind of test and only those who seek personal perfection will survive. If Saturn is afflicted may be overly ambitious and topple from power. Other envious competitors are their testers and attack these people. They can become great administrators without losing perspective of the importance of their own egos. When young they may have conflict with one of their parents to learn compromise and self control. As administrators they learn how to build consensus. Napoleon and Hitler had Saturn in the tenth.

SATURN IN THE ELEVENTH OR AQUARIUS

These individuals focus on developing true friendship, brotherhood and universal welfare. To have friends, one must be friendly. They may suffer from loneliness, neglect, social failure and have trouble finding their place in life. They may have trouble dreaming or rising above material concerns for their own welfare. They may be suspicious of people who seek to be friends and are self conscious in company. Friends may vampirize and use them in social affairs. They learn to be a dependable friend and can see themselves as others see them because they will have friends who are honest and tell them the truth. They need loyal friends.

They are choosy about friends and are not joiners. They can be very ambitious and must learn not to use other people for their own advancement. They are opportunists and need to get over it. It is difficult for them to have a free and easy social exchange. They should be working in humanitarian organizations and have a gift for administration. They should be motivated to work for the good of the group and not by what the group can do for them. They may rebel against committing the self to the welfare of others. They must learn to work for practical, worthwhile goals and enlist the help of stable, older, serious minded people. Karma may come through fanatical adherence to impractical schemes and social expressions. If afflicted, impractical schemes always lead to loss or failure. They may also be slow to adapt to new technology or changes in society.

SATURN IN THE TWELFTH HOUSE OR PISCES

These individuals focus on overcoming self limitations, breaking old habit patterns, and taking self responsibility. People who act to hold them to Saturn's principles act as millstones around their necks. These people stimulate feelings of immaturity, insecurity or inferiority. This can block the flow of life if very severe. They will carry the habit of repression throughout life if they do not work on this consciously. All difficult or disappointing relationships are the result of past life karma. They are the result of not fulfilling self responsibilities and not following the Christ path in dealing with others. They must grow a soul. Now these persons must prove their own worth by facing life's challenges. This manifests as "Somebody out there is at fault" is to be transmuted. These individuals must learn that their motivations have power to shape their destiny. These people don't know who they are or what they are here for until they learn this. One forgets experiences and mistakes are repeated with similar people and scenarios. They must learn to recognize patterns of life consciously and change behaviors to positively shape their environment. They must find strength in lessons from the past and assimilate them. They must face up to their own mistakes and not project them onto someone else. They build inner poise and security by accepting full responsibility for what happens. This is the least objective and down to earth place for Saturn to be in Neptune's house. The person must learn and understand that there are spiritual lessons to be learned in problems. The danger is to become a slave of negative environments. The person allows these to straitjacket them. Sometimes they assume burdens that are not their own. They could become a slave to a chronically ill melancholic mate in a confused martyrdom. Pain often results from failure to adapt to new conditions and continue to live in the past or in a world that could never be. These people have the tendency to retreat to solitude and be left alone. They instead should give themselves in service to help those who are restricted, handicapped or ill while they are rehabilitated. This allows them to think of others' needs instead of dwelling on their own problems.

URANUS KARMIC PATTERN

Uranus is the planet of transformation. Uranus brings changes, sudden, erratic and unpredictable events that break through inertia and set new patterns in motion. Once changes begin, there is no turning back as getting out of ruts sets us free. Structures, attitudes, consciousness of Saturn are examined and transformed. Uranus is the first of the trans-Saturnian planets – Uranus, Neptune, and Pluto – that represent higher consciousness.

Uranus represents the choices of who you want to serve – "Gold vs. God." Are you ready to go beyond logical, material thinking to respond to symbols and patterns through intuition? Instantaneous knowing on inner levels goes beyond linear thinking and leads to creativity and genius.

People with a strong Uranus are original, independent, unconventional, technological, progressive, humanitarian, eccentric, etc. They are interested in all things that are new. Uranians are interested in technology, mechanics, science, engineering, electronics, inventions, space, occultism, alchemy, spirituality, and culture. In regards to personal relationships, they can remain aloof, devoid of heart connections or commitments. There is a desire to be free and independent. They can become very philanthropic with zeal for causes. They can also be ecologically concerned for the earth, plants, animals, forests, oceans, etc.

When Uranus is negatively aspected, it usually indicates selfishness and one-sided views in extreme. Fanaticism and religious intoxication are examples. The Uranian can act to create transformation and change without positive plans or results – such as a terrorist who throws bombs to kill and destroy the status quo. This could mean "Change for change's sake" or "Ends justifying the means."

A retrograde Uranus works on the subconscious levels. A person will delve within themselves to find true values. This can mean seeking self mastery, exhibiting a willingness to transform themselves and then everyone else. They may sense early something they do not like about themselves and can remake their whole personality. They could be humanitarian in thinking that what they find is good for everyone else. They could become the "conscience of the human race" as an agent of change where one can see what values have outlived their usefulness.

Uranians reach beyond polarities of male versus female. An example would be love without the necessity of a partner – friendship. A union is not dependent on emotional bonds between people. Uranians are above possessiveness of things or people. They are true humanitarians and teach by paradoxes. Uranus is the partner of Saturn as Saturn sets up structures and Uranus tears them down to transform crystallizations and dogma. Uranus can transmute materialism into spirituality.

Uranus in the First House or Aries

These individuals focus on transforming their personalities and achieve independence by some unique achievement in their lives. They are encouraged to be themselves in any intimate relationships and can bring new meaning and interest in any new field. They have a restlessness and ambition to do creative things. They have an unusual amount of energy and can be totally consumed in their work. Good examples are those people of the computer industry, scientists, researchers, doctors, etc. who are at the leading edge in their fields. These people are individualists, not followers and must carve out their own paths. They are pioneers and are fueled by excitement and zeal for achievement. The danger is to use their work for personal gain at the expense of others. Their intuitions can be used for crime or immoral applications. Instead, they should use their talents in humanitarian endeavors. Their intuition is flowing directly into their conscious egos.

Uranus in the Second House or Taurus

They want to use their talents to express their uniqueness through their manipulation of personal resources. They can be geniuses in handling money and resources of the earth and become stewards of wealth. This is the opposite of hoarding where resources do not flow. They are not conservative in money matters and have a tendency for speculation where they can use their intuitions. If Uranus is afflicted, their timing may be faulty, acting too quickly without assessing properly, and can lead to losses. Their motives must be clean and not selfish. If not afflicted, they can develop uncanny insight in financial matters. They may have unusual talents that must be developed to creative genius for the benefit of all.

URANUS IN THE THIRD HOUSE OR GEMINI

These individuals must develop a practical, independent use of the mind that is inspired by divine revelation. They have a lively fellowship with all those in their everyday environment. Their minds are very quick and innovative and can be used for scientific or communicative work. If Uranus is afflicting Mercury there can be a danger of scattering the mind and confusion. There may be danger in being accident prone or getting into trouble by what one says without thinking of consequences. There can also be difficulty in communication, speech or mental deficiencies. The mind is running too fast and the will must be developed to slow down and organize the thoughts. This can lead to educational problems and loss of self esteem. If Uranus is not afflicted there can be instantaneous comprehension through intuitive thinking. This type of thinking does not follow step by step solutions. The teacher must still teach step by step logical thinking through the study of mathematics and geometry. This allows thinking from whole to the parts and parts to the whole processes. This brings balance to left and right brain thinking.

URANUS IN THE FOURTH HOUSE OR CANCER

These individuals focus on bringing true values to traditional institutions of family, race, religion, and nationality. They can bring a zest of enjoyment to traditional foundations like the home. They can be happy anywhere in adjusting to changing conditions of their environment. When young there may be difficulty with the parents with no real parent/child relationships. They may rebel and leave home early. They have wanderlust and associate with unusual people in unusual situations. They seek independence by moving around a lot while trying to build home security wherever they may be. No outward security is a fact of life. A positive Uranus brings a keen intuition in evaluating other people's values and expectations. They are quick to change ideas and are very adaptable. End of life situations may be very unsettling.

URANUS IN THE FIFTH HOUSE OR LEO

The individuality is expressed in uninhibited interchange in intimate relationships. They stimulate everyone into deep self discovery. They express independence through dramatic behaviors and situations to shock other people. Examples are found among the celebrities, actors, actresses, and rock stars, etc. They act unconventionally and boldly with a great deal of wastefulness in their expressions. In sexual matters they can be licentious. Many are bisexual or homosexual in their search for pleasure and excitement.

There can be an extreme fluctuation in their emotions and inhibitions. There is a great interest in children. They will have as much interest in other children as much as their own and will allow them much independence. They give freedom in all areas of creativity and expression. Their quest for love is their great adventure. They have the potential to experience true spiritual love. They could fall in love completely on impulse and emotions with completely different types of people than themselves. Their artistic expressions could be very unconventional like Andy Warhol or Picasso.

URANUS IN THE SIXTH HOUSE OR VIRGO

Work is the focus of their self discovery and expression. They have intensely individual work patterns. They have a continuous need to adjust to social conditions. They can bring a sense of adventure to both duty and to work. Negatively they make it impossible for people around them to work. The urge for self reform is very strong. They may come up with creative techniques to apply in their work. Their mind can be put to constructive usage with much skill and ingenuity. They require an unusual vocation to reach beyond conformity. They pride themselves on their unconventional behaviors and innovations. They promote new age ideas on health, nutrition and exercise programs. They can also bring new ideas to union/management or military issues. Uranus afflicted can bring about labor problems, illness, and overwork. The nerves are affected with resulting digestive problems. Intuitive solutions to problems can restore health to the psyche and body if the person uses Uranus positively.

URANUS IN THE SEVENTH HOUSE OR LIBRA

These individuals must express their independence and at the same time assimilate themselves into a harmonious relationship. Challenges coming from marriages and partnerships can bring out their individuality's growth of soul qualities. They may develop an intuitive understanding of others. This can be used constructively as marriage counselors. This may also manifest as unusual marriage agreements and relationships. They may allow their partners a great amount of freedom and demand the same. They will be attracted to unusual people. They may work well with scientists, engineers, aviators, etc. They may also become excellent mediators and bargainers because they can find practical compromises to disagreements. Trines to Uranus indicate that in past lives they have lived and loved much. They can be very useful in working on public reforms in perceptions of others' needs. They can't stand injustice. They may have a large variety of relationships to gain their own spiritual identity. They have a destiny to marry someone who will help them fulfill their own destiny. By helping others to express their own destinies, they fulfill their own potentials in reciprocation. They work best in one to one relationships.

URANUS IN THE EIGHTH HOUSE OR SCORPIO

These individuals express their independence by constantly regenerating themselves. They can manipulate the fruits of relationship in partnerships or marriage to express their individuality. This is the strongest placement for Uranus. They can have instantaneous perceptions using their intuition into other people's emotions, investments, business decisions, and resources of groups and partnerships. They can use the emotions to organize everyone around them. They are mystics by nature and contact other planes of existence through dreams, visions, premonitions and psychic experiences. They have no fears of life and death. They are very resourceful and attract unusual people and situations. They are intense in developing themselves spiritually. When Uranus is afflicted there can be a danger in financial losses and accidents due to recklessness. There may be instability with material concerns with up and down fortunes. There may be financial losses after marriage or regarding legacies. They learn early that karma brings instantaneous returns. They can show genius in solving relationship problems and making perfectly timed investment decisions.

URANUS IN THE NINTH HOUSE OR SAGITTARIUS

They bring reform to religion, philosophy, education, law, travel, and diplomacy. This is how they express their individuality. They are constantly trying to bring understanding to current thought. They require complete freedom of thought. They are able to help anyone think their problems through using their intuition. They have excellent foresight or the gift of prophecy. They make excellent attorneys. They practice "The spirit of the law, and not the letter of the law." They can go beyond precedence to looking at each case individually. If Uranus is afflicted, they can be fanatical in their beliefs and encourage utopian ideas or rebellion. They may have had to gain their education from unconventional sources that are not recognized by orthodox society. They may attract criticism and ostracism for their beliefs or teaching by colleagues fearful of the challenge to their own beliefs.

URANUS IN THE TENTH HOUSE OR CAPRICORN

These individuals exert their individuality through challenges to their authority. They will attract much attention to themselves as they climb professionally. They may have a spectacular life in politics or public affairs. They need to meet enormous numbers of people to establish their power base. They gain much power and responsibility for their constituents. The danger is to use power for their personal gain and fall from power by loss of reputation. They learn to compromise and build consensus. A negatively aspected Uranus brings rebellion against mother, employers, teachers, and authority figures. This leads to instability and the need to change homes and jobs continuously. They may need to be in unstable occupations. They show intolerance to what they view as injustice and are inflexible in their subjective opinions. Those in authority will feel this constant unspoken attack to their authority. The positive contribution of Uranus will be to use power for the benefit of all in creative ways. Their karma is that they have had power in past lives but have not used it properly and became deposed.

URANUS IN THE ELEVENTH HOUSE OR AQUARIUS

These individuals exert their individuality through group power in humanitarian projects. They can be champions of the best of the culture but promote the new and exciting in life. They have organizational talent and bring cooperative power with other people to further society. The bigger the project the more they love it and can pour themselves into it. They are at home in social activities and can be joiners in fraternal or service organizations. They are attracted to unusual people and their friendships change throughout life. They tend to be idealists and social utopians. If Uranus is negative, they can be revolutionaries with impractical causes with rigid views. They can disrupt everyone around them and try to take over organizations to suit their own needs. They may be totally consumed by a cause but neglect their own family responsibilities. They could be devoid of real intimate relationships due to their need for independence. Their karma may be from not caring for the welfare of others in past lives. Their friends may use them for their own selfish ends.

URANUS IN THE TWELFTH HOUSE OR PISCES

In this house of karma intuition must be used to redeem the sins of commission and omission from past lives. They must take responsibility for the effects of the past. Their karma is the karma of extremes. They have been unbalanced, extremists, lawless, and have rebelled against society's conventions. There has been extreme selfishness with an inability to empathize and relate with other people. There has been a misuse of creative energies and loss of reputation. They must grow a soul and must hold themselves responsible for their actions and not blame circumstances or other people. They must face a violent destruction of the crystallization of negative attitudes. They were chronic rebels and could have been imprisoned. They feel as if they are imprisoned and can't accept discipline or restrictions. They would bitterly resent any physical handicaps. Their inner self is being bottled up. On the positive side they can use their intuition to contact the spiritual world. Edgar Cayce had Uranus in the twelfth house. They could be aware of the cause and cure of their own problems and become of great help to heal others of their afflictions. They may take advantage of incoming spiritual influences to use unexpected opportunities that present themselves. They could receive last minute help from the spiritual world when needed most.

NEPTUNE KARMIC PATTERNS

ψ

Neptune is the planet of transcendentalism and illusions. Neptune is the planet of Luciferic temptations versus spirituality. The temptation is to rise above earthly concerns and escape into Nirvana or Utopian states. In the process, one wishes to dissolve into pleasurable nothingness and lose one's individuality. There are often attempts to escape from karma in the flight from responsibility and reality. Neptune is the planet of drugs and alcoholism.

Neptune's highest purposes are reflected as potentials in the sign of Pisces. Here, true spirituality as a channel of spiritual will is guided by the hierarchy of spiritual beings. The ego being endeavors to channel spiritual integrity. This manifests in compassion and endeavors of selfless service to gain understanding of the causes of suffering to humanity, animals, plants, etc. The Buddha brought compassion into the world. There is the desire to align one's self with the Christ path of initiation as an instrument or via transcendentalism.

When Neptune is weak by sign, aspect or placement, it shows misuse of spiritual power. The ultimate perversion is to gain control of other people using spiritualism. Black magic is negative use of inspiration to gain control of another's ego or will. One must seek to be a pure channel.

Neptune can be used to create visions and idealistic representations. Illusions, magic, photographs, motion pictures, virtual reality, video games, storytelling, etc., are examples. Drugs and alcohol are escapes from ego responsibilities. Self-delusions, glamour, charisma, religious intoxications, personality cults, stars of sports, theatre, screen and pop music are all expressions of Neptune's power. It is idealism without reality. Caution and morality are lost for pseudo-spiritual mirages. Mediumship, martyrdom, hypnosis, possession, etc., are other examples.

A retrograde Neptune indicates lessons to be learned in the proper use of the spirit. Karmic returns indicate suffering, sins of omission and commission. Law breaking in the past requires restitution, penance, suffering, confinement, etc., before consciousness is gained to allow the Law of Grace to operate. After the battle between Saturn and Uranus build up structures then tear them down, Neptune comes in to heal the chaos. Neptune dissolves sin and suffering. The choice is to give human service or suffer the consequences. We must try to become an instrument of truth, love and universal compassion without losing individuality.

The idealistic communistic thought is related to Neptune in that everyone loses their individuality and everyone is the same. This is related to the ideals of the Women's Rights movement and related efforts to make equality into sameness. This would dissolve individual culture and make the whole earth one uniform civilization. The temptation is to give up one's individual ego responsibility to the state and be taken care of with no decision making.

This is the opposite of the Principle of Instrumentation in which one surrenders personal will to divine will, to serve as an agency of the release of power. Religion, scientific, artistic and musical expressions are examples of inspiration from the divine. Joan of Arc is an example of divine intervention at the age of nineteen in the saving the French from English domination. In science, Sir Isaac Newton completed his Three Laws of Motion and the accompanying mathematics of calculus by the age of twenty-four. The danger is the perversion of ideals and artistic expressions. This allows destructive astral forces to rise that are impossible to control. An example is the mesmerizing power of Adolph Hitler.

Neptune rules the unconscious mind and indicates where we may redeem unfulfilled ideals and violated divine will. The house position indicates where we have betrayed others for our own selfish purposes. It is also where we have the greatest gifts for healing, compassion and instrumentation.

NEPTUNE IN THE FIRST HOUSE OR ARIES

These individuals have a very difficult incarnation, even with the best of aspects. The body is extremely sensitive to the environment of thought forms, emotional vibrations, poisons and toxins. The body is open to both black and white psychic forces. It is also an indication of a highly developed ego. For these individuals it can be hard to adjust to the practical aspects of life. Neptune is a super passive force. These people can be idealistic dreamers and can be spiritually conscious. Their imaginations are overly active and could distort their outlook and viewpoints and bring on fantasies. Their nervous systems could be very sensitive and delicate. Their persona may be extremely attractive and magnetic with the appearance of sweetness, innocence and purity. At the same time they may have a hard time knowing their own feelings and who they are. An example to study is Marilyn Monroe. Negative aspects may bring karmic return of individuals to test them and their spiritual integrity. They must learn to take responsibility for themselves and trust in the good and positive in life to overcome fears and anxieties of imagined outcomes.

NEPTUNE IN THE SECOND HOUSE OR TAURUS

These individuals must learn to bring inspiration down to practical applications. They can bring excellent taste in designing clothing, landscapes, interiors, buildings, etc. At the same time they may need help in keeping track of money and resources. They have an inability to focus on keeping money as they are lax in financial matters and don't keep accurate accounts. They must learn to neither undervalue nor overvalue material values. They can't become misers or hoarders. Their focus must be on developing their talents as a spiritual obligation to humanity. They must not drop out and become non-earners and welfare recipients. If they work, they will always have sufficient money, sometimes coming in at the last moment.

NEPTUNE IN THE THIRD HOUSE OR GEMINI

The challenge here is to learn to use the inspired mind in practical applications and communication. The mind is continually being inspired and could be put to good use by writing novels or imaginative commentaries. They are very in tuned to the thoughts of other people and can bring lively fellowship to their everyday environment. When Neptune is negatively aspected there can be a lack of mental clarity, memory, or speech. They may have a strange karma with brothers or sisters, may have the burden of caring for them, or they may have mental deficiencies. These individuals can also be very secretive and withdraw from communication due to a mistrust of people in their environment.

They may invade the privacy of neighbors or visa versa. They may confide in the wrong people and become the victims of malicious gossip. They may be confused by misinformation, misdirection and forgotten details and go off in wasteful tangents. There may be situations where they sacrifice needlessly for other people who didn't need it and neglect their own problems. If Neptune is positively aspected they have intuitive insight and tolerance for other people and dedicate themselves to bring understanding to everyone.

NEPTUNE IN THE FOURTH HOUSE OR CANCER

The soul finds refuge in the home, mother, family, and native country. The soul has a subtle sensitivity to the framework of the home that he is born into. The home may be open to a multitude of influences like a meeting place for the discussion of important matters by many people. New spiritual values and spiritual perceptions may be developed in this life. They may have the dream that their home is a veritable utopia or kingdom of god on the earth. These individuals may be very kind and affectionate. They may be very spiritual and influence others favorably through a deep feeling of inner union with other people. They may have the ability to be at home anywhere and can adjust to any conditions. They search for ideals and philosophies they can live by to find freedom in this incarnation. They will not be bound by traditions or external belief systems but feel at peace within themselves in the world. This is not illusions but practical adjustment to life. If Neptune is negatively aspected there may be much suffering and sorrow in the home. The individual may wander in search of security or may drift and try to escape the responsibilities of life. There may be bondage to a hypochondriac parent that demands care or the individual may show this melancholic temperament themselves. This has a tendency to happen in early life or at the end of life. The home atmosphere of habits and patterns may exhibit strange, unreal behaviors. The family may be subject to family scandals, sponging relatives, loss of home through trickery and deceit, or unwise investments. There may be a distortion of values with excessive sentimentality resulting in loss of self and false martyrdom.

NEPTUNE IN THE FIFTH HOUSE OR LEO

The soul's radiance manifests itself with an unearthly charm and charisma. This happens during dynamic confrontations with life with the soul's projection that transcends the physical to the spiritual. The individual exhibits these capacities for self expression through art, music and drama with an abundance of enthusiasm, idealism, and joy. There may be an inexhaustible source of imagination which the individual can draw upon. Children with this placement may have active imaginations or imaginary playmates and must be nurtured with kindness. They may be gifted or unusual. Love affairs may be a search for the ideal partner and can bring much happiness. Creative talents must be developed with discipline and regular work patterns. When Neptune is used negatively creative energies bring illusions, selfishness, and wastefulness leading to disappointment and suffering. Otherworldly glamour can lead to a constant search for true love beyond the sensual. This can lead to a wanton pursuit of pleasure and excitement in romance. Another danger is to succumb to gambling and speculative excesses.

NEPTUNE IN THE SIXTH HOUSE OR VIRGO

In these individuals the sense of service is idealized and they may have a mysterious gift of healing. They can serve everyone with a keen social instinct to know what people need. They have a very good ability to plan for the future but need attention to details without negligence or laxity from themselves or co-workers. They may accept any task and exhaust themselves in working too long and hard. They are driven by duty or obligation and must develop a fair division of work and not allow others to be lazy. They must watch that their own health does not deteriorate and fail. They must not become martyrs through self imposed slavery to conditions. They must impose self discipline and routine and orderly work patterns. They may need vocational counseling to find meaningful work where they are duly rewarded for their efforts.

NEPTUNE IN THE SEVENTH HOUSE OR LIBRA

These individuals have a mystical need to believe in others. They will project their souls to another and have it mirrored back to them. They have the tendency to idealize close relationships and at the same time to not see them clearly. The true details of the other person are lost in illusion. These persons will have broad associations but may float over them and not really incarnate in them. They have concern for larger issues such as the quality and value of their contact with the other person. They may not be able to see the needs of the partner. They may have symbolic relationships and not really earthly ones. The end results may be noble but tragic. Relationships require critical evaluation. All permanence in human relationships may be denied. There may be peculiar deceptions in marriage or partnerships. Relationships must be lived with spiritual honesty and faith. A danger will be to blend with another and lose the individuality and become all things to all people. They may have the destiny to marry a very unusual person that is very spiritual or a seer. Or they may have a great desire to salvage a lost soul, to save, uplift, or reform a weak character. One can be very inspirational to the other person but the partner must be willing to respond and improve themselves. A word of caution for these people is to read the fine print of legal contracts and avoid all legal entanglements.

NEPTUNE IN THE EIGHTH HOUSE OR SCORPIO

These people must bring practicality to financial matters involving money or the resources of others. There is danger in laxity in the financial affairs in dealing with other people. Agreements that are made are not lived up to or are not clear leading to misunderstandings. All agreements should be in writing. Common resources of partnerships or marriages require care and reality. Financial schemes may bring bubbles that burst and end as a mess of confusing entanglements. They may be the result of unsound speculative investments, gullibility, or deceit. This position also rules intricate dealing with banking, insurance, corporate finance, estates and legacies, and taxation. Orderly bookkeeping is required for integrity of tax audits. These people learn about financial interdependence, loans, credit, welfare, and public assistance. These people may be creative financing geniuses. They have the ability to be self sustaining or caring for vast sums of money obtained through inheritance. They may be very compassionate and philanthropic and have the ability to accept inevitable changes and can transition to new patterns when old patterns have outlived usefulness. They are very adaptable to new standards of value and can salvage the best of the past to rise like the phoenix from the ashes. These individuals can contact spiritual beings from other planes of existence.

NEPTUNE IN THE NINTH HOUSE OR SAGITTARIUS

These individuals strive for the highest planes of thought. Abstract thought is idealized and illumines the path to wisdom and aspirations.

Symbols, mandalas, and mazes are utilized to penetrate into the meaning of the archetypes. They are adept at gaining through travel both physically and mentally through actual or vicarious experience. They are full of wishes, plans, and ideas spanning the universe. They are receptive to mystical experiences and are reformers in religious, educational, legal, and social welfare fields. The danger is to be impractical dreamers that do a great deal of talk but do not translate their ideas into deeds.

NEPTUNE IN THE TENTH HOUSE OR CAPRICORN

These individuals strive for worldly achievement in the professional or political life. They wish to find a reflection of their own soul in the outer life. They wish to bring their mystical ideals into reality. They may do this through the creative arts or in humanitarian endeavors. They bring a high standard to their work. They are involved in community building efforts where diverse elements are brought to together. They may be dominated by a collective karma as a channel for group interests. Leadership is based on the consciousness soul, building consensus for group decisions; but the group members may not be ready for this. This must be in the public realm and must be continuously established and renewed. At their best they dramatize the values of the humanity and dignity of man. They may be the victim of public criticism by those lacking in their own development and understanding. They are always in danger of scandal and slander and must sometimes violate established codes as they endeavor to apply transcendental values in the world. This may bring problems in relationships with superiors who are threatened by such radical ideas. Career matters will appear baffling to these people. They will be tested to uphold their own standards and move on or to compromise. They may over or under value their own contributions causing anxiety and uncertainty in professional matters. They may not get promotions that are warranted. They may do better to influence authority from behind the throne and not be exposed to the public eye. They could have position without power or they may attain power very easily with a great gift for being at the right place at the right time. There can be strange circumstances in regards to power and position.

NEPTUNE IN THE ELEVENTH HOUSE OR AQUARIUS

These individuals bring idealism to humanitarian social movements to uphold culture and the best that society values. They attract friendships of high quality to participate in worthy causes. They act as channels for encouraging all idealistic goals for mankind. The capacity for friendship is expressed with no strings attached. They can give inspirational and spiritual support to all friends. They have a strange power of attraction for unusual people with rare and extraordinary friendships as a result. They can share noble aims and aspirations and can work toward their realization. They have psychic ability with imagination and true perceptive insight into other people and events. The danger is to be undiscriminating in the choice of friends and associations and to be dependent on the encouragement of others with wishful thinking. They can fall prey to seduction, falsehood, and fraud. They may idealize friends and choose and confide in the wrong people. They may be too easily diverted from their own ideals and goals. Or they may be disruptive to organization that they join.

Neptune in the twelfth house or Pisces

These individuals focus on redeeming unfulfilled ideals in themselves and in mankind. They act as beacons of light to reveal the divine and dignity of man. Their inner life is open to spiritual influences and can be the source of all wisdom and spiritual insight. All past lifetimes seem to be channeled into this lifetime. They can find answers to all problems and are sustained by power drawn upon when needed. They gain by seclusion and meditation and prayer. They have a belief in the fundamental goodness of life. If Neptune is acting negatively they can be prone to delusion, self doubt, and passivity. They suffer from the misrepresentation of spiritual truth and become assailed by karmic return of people they have wronged in the past. There can be much suffering, death, and heartbreak with confusion on why things are happening to them. They may need confinement or illness, accidents or handicaps to allow them to contemplate why they must activate their will to improve and make amends. Their experiences in life may be harrowing and disconcerting while all efforts at psychological assurance are denied. They must learn to follow the Christ path and build faith.

PLUTO KARMIC PATTERNS

♇

The Greek god Hades and the Roman god Pluto is the ruler of the underworld and the dead. This god controls the vast riches of the earth: gold, silver, platinum, iron, coal, uranium, oil, etc. His queen is Persephone, who brings spring to earth after spending winter in the underworld. Pluto is the symbol of the great seeding process, which is the guarantor of immortality. Seeds must proceed into the depths to germinate just as the Christ descended to Hades for three days before ascending to earth with illumination. Pluto is the solar seed of the solar system and spends eleven out of two hundred and forty-nine years inside the orbit of Neptune, bringing changes to the course of human history by bringing to consciousness impulses from the depths of man's subconscious. Though far from the Sun's light, Pluto has great power to transform life on Earth. Pluto's purpose helps us realize the God within our own depths and make our souls something real, concrete and redeemed. Man can become the perfected microcosm and return to the macrocosm. Pluto brings release from the past and fulfillment of new beginnings. It burns racial karma as, through diversity, all become one. Pluto is the planet of transformation and rebirth. Pluto works through the Resonance Principle in which repetitive processes initiate a sequence of conditions that build up over a period of time that obscures the initiating process. It can bring catastrophic results, like atomic fission. Atomic fission can be controlled by lead which is the metal of Saturn. Karma holds transformation in check through development of Saturn's virtues. Pluto can also promote the disintegration of the personality in schizophrenia or the proliferation of cancer cells.

Pluto also works through the Principle of Banishment in which things are brought to a halt and are never resumed. Friendships that exhibit a strange love/hate dynamic may end or last a lifetime. Pluto will cleanse the subconscious of all false layers to show what the person really is. Then we can see ourselves as a part of the greater whole. Pluto's purpose is to disintegrate falseness and temptations. Pluto can annihilate human feelings and self respect, excuse brute force, aggrandize lust and torture and allow animal instincts to come to the surface. Pluto can subjugate human freedom by disregarding the importance of the individual's ego. Laws are made to enforce the distrust of the individual.

A retrograde Pluto guarantees that the individual will have to work on the self to eliminate all negative aspects of the soul. The house position will indicate in what department of life the challenges will present themselves. There could be deep seated fears and phobias arising from the unconscious. First there are feelings of emptiness, and we delve into ourselves to rid ourselves of false shells in which we used to find security.

PLUTO IN THE FIRST HOUSE OR ARIES

These individuals must deal with excessive inferiority complexes. They don't have control of themselves and are not their own master. They may have an excessive ego or timidity. They have a tendency to over or underestimate themselves. Their psychic energies may be drawn back into the subconscious. If this person discovers his/her true identity they can act as a true channel for others. Ambition and power will be expressed in leadership and they appear to have a will of their own. They may wield great influence in social or political affairs. They could isolate themselves from society and be banished or they may banish undesirable people from their lives. They may find that personal activities and interests may suddenly be brought to a halt, and when life is renewed they may take a completely different tack. This is especially true when Pluto has negative aspects. They may act as a channel for karmic forces working toward universal brotherhood and welfare. They may undergo a complete personality change throughout life. Their thoughts will determine the changes as the person will become what he/she thinks and feels as the mind has power.

PLUTO IN THE SECOND HOUSE OR TAURUS

In this house and sign Pluto tends to destroy feelings of worldly security. They may have an obsession to find security and fear an excessive outflow of material resources or money. They could be denied financial rewards for their efforts or they could be self denying or self sacrificing. They may surrender their possessions to follow spiritual causes or pursuits. Or they may amass wealth. They may begin a business from scratch and build it into a huge enterprise. They have a tremendous interest in value and could have a talent for dealing with money and possessions. The self may become obsessed with what it owns or what they have is less important than what they want. Gaining new possessions brings them self esteem. These individuals may go through a periodic stripping of possessions to learn spiritual values. Once you lose everything you begin to understand true values. They must learn to be stewards of resources for the benefit of all.

Pluto in the third house or Gemini

These individuals face challenges of the mind and communications. They may find it difficult to concentrate and speak clearly their thoughts. Or they may have a great ability to concentrate and to speak with power and clarity. They may have the ability to influence through propaganda and the media. There could be apathy or an overexcitement intellectually. There could be a dispersion of mental powers, mental deficiency, or an inability to communicate clearly. The thoughts could run too fast for words or to get facts clearly. There may be difficulty in reading or writing as the will must be tamed. On the positive side they may challenge and question all superficial and obsolete modes of thinking. They want to regenerate the psyche and participate in an uncompromising effort to plumb the very depths of the consciousness. They could have a strong analytical interest in everyday relationships or they may have life or death struggles with brothers and sisters. They could ferret out the best of social capabilities of all people they may deal with. They may enjoy intellectual entertainment, question and answer games, puzzles, etc. Or they may become addicted to the computer and internet.

Pluto in the fourth house or Cancer

These individuals are challenged to find the center of their being that is invulnerable to personal earthquakes. Only in the deepest roots can this person find stability in life. If they are shaken through their emotions then all objectivity is lost. They are perpetually in search of security. These persons are strongly hampered by family and past life ties to family members. They could see their home as a disappointment, regardless of what the home is like. Their emotional maturity is hampered. The mother will tie this person to family problems and paralyze the emotions. The soul is corroded by self doubt, religious, hereditary or racial issues. The parents could stimulate one's deepest fears and be removed from them early. The home could be destroyed or abandoned. These people will be driven to establish the security of the home. They would make good researchers, scientists, mining engineers, psychologists, geologists, or archeologists that bring things to the surface. At age seven there could be a crisis of the deep feelings. Favorable aspects to Pluto would modify home conditions to beneficial changes. It could also lead to extreme old age and good care. They could be placed in the role of counseling others and could be the beginning of a new cycle having to do with human welfare.

Pluto in the fifth house or Leo

These individuals are driven to control their emotional intensity and creative self expression. They have an intense personal need for emotional satisfaction. There is an exuberant outflow of emotional intensity that can drain the self. There can be a cyclone of unfulfilled desires to love and be loved. They make an in depth self discovery and will take risks to dramatize their personality. Life will bring intense distractions in life of dangerous enterprises where there is the thrill of risk. They may go globe trotting for ecological or humanitarian causes. Their own children may need to take risks and challenges and become a rebel to their parents. These persons can be thrown off center through intense sexual or emotional expression. They experiment with unconventional love and family relationships because they want to go their own way. They may have an exuberant confidence and think they can do anything without anyone's advice. They can bring new dimensions to people's consciousness. Or they can choose to be wasteful, banish themselves from society and drop out and encourage others to do the same. Their romantic affections may seem to be casual but they are very deeply felt. Creative self expressions are best channeled into drama, art, and music. They can produce bizarre expressions or very unusual, powerful and accomplished children. They may be fascinated by the macabre, monsters, or horror stories. They may be attracted to take risks in gambling or speculation and have spectacular gains or losses. Destiny may play a part in changing profits into losses such as stock market crashes or wars. If Pluto is afflicted there could be a danger of sexual attack, abortions, prostitution, etc.

PLUTO IN THE SIXTH HOUSE OR VIRGO

These individuals feel that they have not been successful with their creative self expressions (Leo) and now are driven to self improvement through a choice of two paths. They are devotion, or following ideals in their daily lives, or discipleship in which they follow the disciplines given them by a religious leader. Eventually they must follow the maxim, "Serve or suffer" in their quest for self redemption. Since Pluto here affects through the mind and nervous system they may be subject to illness of the mind, obsessions, psychosomatic anxieties, mental confusion, lapses of memory, morbid or depressing thoughts, etc. Lack of self confidence is the result with the drive to improve. On the physical level the lungs and digestion are affected or they may be susceptible to allergies or virus infections. They could have fevers, infections, or disorders of the blood. They may be afflicted by work related illnesses such as radiation poisoning, black lung disease, asbestos, mercury, or accidents. They must have periodic medical checkups to avoid being caught by surprise. These individuals want to know how to be of service and are challenged by social or working conditions, employees or coworkers. They may be perfectionists and demand too much of themselves or others. They may suffer banishment from their work. Conditions may change and their jobs may disappear. On the positive side they may be involved in promoting union workers rights or contract negotiations. They must watch out for unreliable or deceptive persons. They may be overconfident about their ability to reform others or in the abilities of others. They must watch also for becoming too myopic and rely on regimentation or conformity. It is possible for these individuals to become excellent researchers or practitioners in the health fields where they help people who help themselves.

PLUTO IN THE SEVENTH HOUSE OR LIBRA

The challenge here is to make in depth self transformation through establishing balanced marriages and partnerships. One strives for cooperation, empathy, and harmony through unselfish blending with the partner. The separateness of two becomes the union of one. One partner may have to relinquish home and family ties for the good of the marriage. Individual hopes and wishes for the marriage will gradually fade away. If afflicted aspects hold sway the partner's unwise words or actions will bring about dissolving of bonds. This will bring about misunderstandings and lack of rapport resulting in loneliness. Partners may disappear or die but the person left behind will be left holding responsibilities of bills, children, etc. These people may be drawn into dealing with the underworld or with very powerful people. They may be subjected to another's will through domination and negativity and find themselves in a battle for survival. They may be forced into a karmic marriage where the emotions rule reason. Irrational and instinctive forces work to destroy the bonds between one person and another. Relationships can be love/hate or life/death in intensity challenging the individuality. The partner can be banished or can be held in a lifelong relationship. Unconscious negative aspects of the self will arise and must be cleansed from the soul. The person may begin by avoiding any close relationships but once it gets going they will find themselves in an intense whirlwind of adjustment. After surviving these challenges these individuals make excellent marriage or psychological counselors or negotiators.

Pluto in the eighth house or Scorpio

These individuals are challenged to control their emotional intensity in adjusting to close relationships with partners or groups. They will be involved with handling group resources or the resources of others. They are attracted to business, bankruptcies, investments, estates, insurance, taxes, salvage, finance, etc. They make excellent investigators, detectives, secret service agents, executors, brokers, etc. They ferret out hidden information and use it to their advantage. Like James Bond (007), they can be ruthless in carrying out their assignments. As surgeons they can be precise but unemotionally detached. They are distrustful of other people's motives and values. They like to be independent and trust their own rules and values but tend to follow societal or institutional directives. This is their dilemma. They may use sex or money as their weapons. Their emotions experience the extremes of highest to lowest. They are open to astral influences or can be channels when aligned to good spiritual influences. They can bring spiritual healing to the emotional life of others. Their life habits are built around the desires of others and there could be fanaticism. They are attracted to powerful or extravagant people or the military where there are life and death risks. They may be involved with organized crime. For some, there may be mystery involved in their deaths. They may disappear and their cause of death will be unknown. Their deaths may be experienced entirely alone or in groups. Watch for violence with negative aspects to Mars, Uranus, or Neptune. Karma is from misuse of sexual forces or occult power.

PLUTO IN THE NINTH HOUSE OR SAGITTARIUS

These individuals seek to be involved with groups of intellectual or religious affinity. They may identify themselves with past epics of human history and historical figures of that era. This may be a remembrance of a past incarnation. They have a desire to expand and understand one's involvement in the larger aspects of life. They have a driving insistence on knowing in depth and not being superficial. They can infect others with enthusiasm. They can become symbolic figures and become beacons of light to guide others. They are fated to incarnate some deep principle of human existence through their example. Their best expression is to elevate the standards of the society. They strive for the unattainable in knowledge, to completely understand the human condition. This requires extensive travel and study. They make excellent anthropologists, researchers, teachers, journalists and lecturers. They require a scientific educational approach to keep them grounded in reality. They attract challenges and opposition from others and if Pluto is acting negatively they invite banishment and exile as others won't listen. They can feel more and more isolated as they get deeper and deeper into knowledge. They have the danger of becoming demagogues and try to impose their beliefs on others. They may have problems with teachers when studying higher education. When Pluto acts positively they can go very deeply into ancient age teachings and will remain nonsectarian in their approach knowing all religions and philosophies. They may have exceptional writing abilities that are profound and extensive. Their knowledge will be spiritually inspired to communicate to the masses.

When they are young they will have a strong propensity to inquire into various religions and will spend a lifetime studying different religions and philosophies. They can bring about a complete regeneration of their consciousness. Self integration will take place in the mind and will eliminate past conditioning of thoughts of society. Spiritual development will make possible travel on the astral plane consciously. There will be deeper understanding of reincarnation brought in from wisdom of past incarnations.

PLUTO IN THE TENTH HOUSE OR CAPRICORN

The challenges facing these individuals is transformation of the self while adjusting to the career or their established place in the world. They have great sensitivity to misuse of power. One's projection into outer life has many obstacles. It begins in childhood with misunderstandings with the parents creating feelings of ingratitude which promotes hostility. Later on it is with those in authority. Instinctive hostile forces can be sensed by superiors. Promotions can be held back. These individuals must learn lessons of diplomacy and patience. These individuals are born revolutionaries who challenge superficialities of the human race through activism. They can demonstrate ruthlessness in their acts that can eventually involve the whole world. They can project themselves totally into career or political involvements in large undertakings. They have an untiring struggle for recognition, power, and independence while winning a great deal of support of their group. Their danger is to misuse group power. Their position in public life can come to a stop and they can be banished from power with the loss of reputation and the support of their group. Changes will be reflected in the outer life from changes within. Circumstances will appear to be beyond the person's conscious control. They must go within to put their inner resources in order for their next ascent. If they survive the challenges then circumstances will improve and will be supporting. These are the times when they must exhibit to their utmost their initiative, integrity, honor, courage, and innate abilities. An example is Winston Churchill after being thrown out of office and awaiting his return to power during World War II. If there are many negative aspects to Pluto there will be insecurity of the ego with challenges to their business interests and social position leading to a constant desire for change and improvement. Destiny operating under Pluto makes the person compelled to follow whatever circumstances that arise. When out of office, Winston Churchill had to come to America to lecture to ease his monetary debts. He had Scorpio on the tenth house and Pluto in the third which gave him great oratory powers. These individuals could be political geniuses and act as channels to bring about world changes. They may be estranged from their parents in early life and have no normal home life which will make them self dependent and make their own way in life. They turn inward and accept inner guidance with faith in their destinies.

Pluto in the eleventh house or Aquarius

These individuals will have challenges to transform the self by working closely with friends and group associates in worthy causes for the benefit of humankind. The average person will be driven willfully to fulfill mass conditions, hopes, wishes, rewards, and friendships that occur every day in the mundane world. Once the struggle with the lower self has been won, a very great talent for self good by human service may be utilized. These people need a wide circle of friends and acquaintances to increase their consciousness to make them more humanitarian. Social and business relationships from the highest to the lowest levels of society are needed for self development. They can become great leaders with devotion to high ideals. They will have powerful friends with Sun conjunction to Pluto. They will have aspirations to do great things to change conditions of society for the better of everyone. They are never satisfied with their aspirations. This is a favorable house for scientific and occult studies. The orthodox sciences will be expanded to spiritual sciences. Small beginnings will lead to huge expansions of all levels.

When Pluto is used negatively, friends must be chosen carefully. They may speak too freely to their friends about their plans, goals, and aspirations and thus losing power of will. Other people will then try to help them achieve their goals and eventually completely change the relationship. Friends can completely change to become enemies. These individuals must watch that dwelling on their own hopes and wishes do not have a destructive effect. If they do well they may think too much and change their thinking about their goals after they have achieved them, then they go on to bigger goals. They may lose social perspective and think they have moved beyond their friends and deliberately break the bonds of friendship. Due to different rates of growth, interests may change leading to banishment. Friends can be lost through some inexorable blow of fate. Since this is in the Aquarius house there is a lack of emotionalism and too much intellectualism. Personal relationships can be neglected and the love life can be out of balance with partners and children. They can be sacrificed for higher ideals, selfishness, stubbornness, and lack of perspective. There is also the danger of placing the goals of big enterprises to obtain profits and success above spiritual values and the welfare of the common man. This only leads to frustration if the self is the primary consideration.

PLUTO IN THE TWELFTH HOUSE OR PISCES

These individuals must redeem their soul of karmic past life acts of commission and omission. Unconscious forces will arise to bring to consciousness aspects of the soul that must be examined and must be responsibly acknowledged as to fault. Deep and obsessive desires will come to the surface through other people and events. The relentless enemy exhibits as guilt complexes, fears and phobias. The soul has difficulty in manifesting its own light. These individuals may not have wished to be incarnated at this time and have a very strong feeling that there is something wrong. They may have difficulty in submitting to rules of life and to live within these rules. They wish to live above karmic law as they consciously broke karmic laws in the past. They are bringing to a conclusion a cycle of lives where they have been transmuting this law breaking karma. They may act as a karmic agent by stirring up fateful events in the lives of people around them. They can get their friends to change and break down old karmic patterns. Karmic forces are released to promote constructive forces of self transformation. Any weakness to not follow karmic law will bring suffering and unhappiness. Tempters will arise so they must stand firm. Selfishness in action, thought or speech will cause others to retaliate with vengeance. The desire to exploit others will lead to restrictions, banishment, and isolation. This may manifest as conviction for criminal activities of sex slavery, prostitution, smuggling, drugs, black market activities, or murder. These individuals can't escape their karma. If there are good aspects to planets in the sixth or tenth houses to Pluto in the twelfth, karma can be sublimated through law enforcement and work through service. There can be a daily experience of seeing how people suffer through lawlessness. They may experience how medical, psychological, remedial corrections, etc. can redeem karma. When there is a conscious and deliberate attempt to give oneself in service then beneficial events can enter to help them reclaim lost souls and redeem their own soul and astral body. Trines to Pluto in the twelfth indicate these individuals have brought in the fruits of past psychic development and have many talents to be given to the world. They may want to live in seclusion to work in metaphysical realms of consciousness for the benefit of humanity.

MOON'S NODES AND INTERCEPTIONS

☊

THE MOON'S NODES

The Moon's Nodes are formed where the intersection of the plane of the Moon's orbit around Earth intersects the plane of Earth's orbit around the Sun. These two points of interception are called the Moon's Nodes. When the Moon rises from below the plane of the ecliptic it is called the North Node of the Moon, and where the Moon falls below the plane of the ecliptic it is called the South Node of the Moon. When the Moon is conjunct one of its nodes, it is called an eclipse. The lunar sphere is the home of the spiritual hierarchy called Angels, which are one level above humanity and are responsible on a personal level for each human being. When the Moon contacts the North Node it opens cosmic or spiritual influences. It represents the symbol of Hermes, two serpents coiling around a staff. The South Node is associated with fate or karma. Together this axis of fate indicates where cosmic energies enter and exit into individual consciousness since it relates to our relationship to others or the society. The North Node brings new material for the individual to work on to build his/her destiny by training our will in this lifetime. We must use our will to become an assertive force for the future. We cannot depend on karma or the past but we must take up the opportunities of the present. We can receive the maximum spiritual return if we develop our will. It is our responsibility to pick and choose what we bring into our consciousness to transform our experiences into wisdom. This process builds self integration and a true individual. When potentials are fully realized then they become a source of power and protection. The position of house and sign indicate where the positive focus of our consciousness can be manifested. Therefore, the North Node of the Moon can indicate our life's work or vocational opportunities.

The South Node represents the pull of the past. It pertains to habits and talents that are easy to rely upon and repeating. In some way we know that if we do not develop new faculties we can't be personally fulfilled. We can alleviate insecurity and fear of the South Node by consciously working on the North Node character traits. We may feel insecure and uncertain at first but as we gain confidence in our new abilities anxiety is relieved. If talents are expended too much they become the person's Achilles heel.

The Nodal axis moves in a retrograde motion that takes 18.6 years to complete a cycle. The Nodes are reversed every 9.3 years producing opportunities for destiny or ego consciousness to arise. For example, at 9.3 years we feel ourselves as separate individuals with personal responsibilities for our lives. We realize that we are mortal. We realize that our parents are mortal and are not infallible. At 18.6 years, we choose in which vocational direction we will choose to pursue. At 27.9 years, which corresponds to the Point of Self returning to the Ascendant, we take up responsibility for our own life destiny.

NODES AND THE PLANETS

NORTH NODE CONJUNCT MOON

This individual is strongly influenced by their mother or a substitute mother image. A strong reliance on the mother may be transformed into a capacity to adjust to circumstances. There is a strongly developed capacity to feel one's way through life. This can be a sheer opportunism where behaviors are developed by pure convenience. They have tact, diplomacy and an understanding of people. They have the ability to give psychological help to people as well as to a disordered society. Negatively, they may not reach emotional maturity and still be dependent on their mothers.

SOUTH NODE CONJUNCT MOON

The mother's influence is strong, but there is a tendency to repudiate the mother's influences. The mother's influence is transformed into a transcendent psychic image of religion or psychic experiences. There is a powerful urge to be a mother of physical or intellectual children. There are definite talents for acting as a mother. There may be a karmic bondage with the mother.

MOON SQUARE TO THE FATE AXIS

The moon is at the maximum northern or southern latitude and is the maximum point of discord. The ability to handle problems of adjustment to everyday life is at a minimum. The individual is too subjective.

NORTH NODE CONJUNCT MID-HEAVEN (1 DEGREE ORB)

There is a compulsive individual drive for a personal destiny as a public servant.

SOUTH NODE CONJUNCT MID-HEAVEN (1 DEGREE ORB)

This individual will sacrifice the self to a public destiny with a creative release of talent as an administrator or public servant. The life will be controlled by destiny. There may be a special capacity for ego integration in this life.

NORTH NODE CONJUNCT ASCENDANT AND DESCENDANT

There is a strong life emphasis on developing consciousness and identity. There is a talent in forming and keeping partners and relationships.

SUN CONJUNCT NORTH NODE

These individuals move toward self mastery through power, will, and purpose. Power must be used with love or there will be a perversion of power by extreme egotism and domination of others. There can be joyous self expression or self integration.

SUN CONJUNCT SOUTH NODE

Power is easily used for domination or mastery over others.

MERCURY CONJUNCT NORTH NODE

These individuals make creative use of the intellect. They have a capacity for planning and organizing one's time and energy to build for mental development needed for self development. They may be forced into development of writing and speaking skills.

Mercury conjunct South Node

These individuals must learn proper utilization of the mind. Misuse causes problems in thinking and communication. The thinking can block out the emotions.

Venus conjunct North Node

The soul is encouraged and stimulated to develop in this lifetime through relationships and love. This can include refinement through the arts and esthetic development. There can be harmonious attitudes towards others with tact, sympathy, justice, diplomacy and the development of all social graces.

Venus conjunct South Node

These individuals have facility is expressing love, harmony and co-operation in relationships. The danger is to prostitute the self to gain security and money.

Mars conjunct North Node

These people experience a healthy movement towards a constructive life pattern with courage, initiative, responsibility, and the right use of one's energy. They develop through work and self directed activity. They have idealism, faith, and determination to overcome limitations and handicaps.

Mars conjunct South Node

These people are fighters for causes or idealistic goals. The danger is to be wild and irresponsible in the focus of one's energies. There may be a loss of security to gain perspective of values.

Jupiter conjunct North Node

Life urges these people to develop good fellowship and stability. They give themselves in improving conditions outside of themselves.

They are aware of spiritual, moral and religious laws. They exhibit kindness, benevolence, optimism, giving and forgiving, and generosity.

Jupiter conjunct South Node

They have been givers in the past but too much has led to undoing. They need to develop discrimination and discretion in their efforts to do good deeds and gain respectability. The danger is their gullibility.

Saturn conjunct North Node

These people are encouraged to develop a sense of responsibility and maturity through patience to overcome frustrations and limitations. They must learn to accept their own limitations and learn from past mistakes. They must learn practicality in the use of things of the earth. They learn through the acceptance of life's responsibilities and karma.

Saturn conjunct South Node

They have been very responsible persons in the past. These individuals strive towards perfection and have difficulty in accepting themselves with any limitations or imperfections.

Uranus conjunct North Node

These individuals are encouraged in life to seek liberation from bondage to orthodox thought and conditions. They must move into progressive thought. They are led to decrystalize habit patterns that have grown outdated or are now blocking progress and must be thrown out. They are moving toward utilizing intuitive powers.

Uranus conjunct South Node

There is a talent for decrystalizing orthodoxy. There is a compulsive breaking of old patterns and bonds. Old rules and laws must be replaced with constructive new ones.

Neptune conjunct North Node

These persons are led into spiritual development and develop a humanitarian consciousness of compassion and idealism. They can develop faculties of becoming a spiritual channel to bring inspiration through art, music, drama, etc.

Neptune conjunct South Node

There will be evidence of past psychic development and a facility to work with people using compassion and understanding. The danger is to use these talents for selfish purposes. There is a liability to possession and obsessions with displacement of the ego.

Pluto conjunct North Node

These individuals have psychological abilities to deal with the deep unconscious mind. They are developing a universal viewpoint that is personally integrated. This includes occult and mystical integration. They are concerned with universal welfare and all systems of higher thought integrated into a universal philosophy. The development of the higher mind is the impulse for development in this life. They delve into the depths of the self to find the God within. They can totally regenerate and transform the personality self into the Higher Self where they are invulnerable to challenges.

Pluto conjunct South Node

They have past spiritual power and development. They have facility in becoming spiritual leaders. They have the danger of overestimation of their power and become inclined to break karmic laws.

North Node in the Houses and Signs

North Node in the first house or Aries

These individuals learn from experiences in which they have made a personal stand. They must develop their own personality and stand on their own decisions. They have an ease in relating to others and have a danger of becoming dependent on others. They do allow their partners to develop ease or grace of personality. They can win cooperation from other people very easily. They can also become involved in competitive situations with other people. The danger is to become involved in so many relationships that this person becomes a slave to other people.

They must learn to be self initiating and develop a personal goal in this lifetime.

NORTH NODE IN THE SECOND HOUSE OR TAURUS

The basic problem is to learn to manage the things that they own. This includes their power, talents, resources, mental faculties and possessions. Good management on the personal level ensures good rewards from partnerships. Banking too much on the resources of their partners will bring self undoing. They must stress their own traditions and background rather than relying on others or trusting in them too implicitly. Their earning power is good but they must learn to be good stewards of their wealth. They can be tempted to become reckless in investments. Another danger is to neglect mindfulness in the buildup of debts.

NORTH NODE IN THE THIRD HOUSE OR GEMINI

This has to do with developing the practical use of the mind in everyday situations. They must learn to think concretely and evaluate situations correctly. They need to establish the relationships between facts in the everyday life. With the South Node in the ninth, they may try to escape from the everyday practical world thinking and get lost in abstract thinking. Their thoughts are religious, mystical, occult, and philosophical. They must bring abstracts down into writing and communications. They have a flair for everyday personal contacts and can be very persuasive. These people can be intellectually curious and require a tremendous education or equivalent reading or self study. They have an innate disrespect for formal education and may drop out. They can be lifelong students seeking innovative solutions and answers to the riddles of life.

NORTH NODE IN THE FOURTH HOUSE OR CANCER

The home and family are the foundation for their personality development. They are building a deep soul foundation on a higher level through meditation. They fight the tendency to be motivated by prestige and good opinion by others. If there is too much egotism then they have the karmic possibility to lose prestige. There may be a compulsion to be a leader in the public realm and they may have a flair for administration.

North Node in the Fifth House or Leo

They have a need to develop self expressive talents. Their personality is on stage as they exhibit creativity, emotional power, and intensity. They need children or some other creative outlet. If this need is satisfied then social activities bring fruitful activity. They can be excellent teachers, artists or inventors. They have empathy for young people. They strive to express some form of leadership in a creative field of self expression. If they are frustrated this leads to emotional frustrations and disruptive relations with friends. They make friends easily but must learn to discriminate in their choice of friends and goals. They must not depend on friends too much but must develop the self. They must deal with their emotionalism and tendency to sensationalism as instinctual habits.

North Node in the Sixth House or Virgo

These individuals are hard at work developing the mastery of techniques. Their experiences are related to self improvement. If their will and endurance are adequate then personal growth from crisis will bring great benefits. There is great suffering to learn humility. They will overcome psychological problems and learn to deal with psychosomatic issues. They may follow a spiritual teacher in a life of devotional service. Their self undoing is through compulsive introspection. They are too self concerned. They may have a passive attitude and drift along with the tide. The advanced soul has a tendency towards developing the inner life through meditation or could have a fateful involvement with social causes through self sacrifice. They may have had much spiritual development in the past and are attuned to inner guidance and protection. Self isolation and hermit like instincts must be replaced by working in the world.

North Node in the Seventh House or Libra

The challenge is to work on building good relationship consciousness. They must learn to integrate themselves through a close relationship and to relate to society also. One must find one's place as a productive member of society. One learns to define roles of masculine versus feminine polarities. The South Node in the first house conjunction to the ascendant gives ego charm and a good personality that can be misused for selfish purposes. These persons must learn to empathize and to relate.

NORTH NODE IN THE EIGHTH HOUSE OR SCORPIO

The challenge is to learn to surrender the ego to the partnership. This requires the blending of two individuals into one entity. Partners and business partners teach you to manage joint resources and individual possessions. There will be transactions on business and emotional levels. You will experience the surrendering one's ego to the partnership. These individuals may experience being swallowed up in a large business corporation. They could be drawn into a deep study of the occult in karmic relationships, life and death issues, hidden forces of nature, regeneration, or spiritual rebirth. Self undoing comes through financial talents and facility, great wealth, or mishandling of funds. These individuals may exhibit resilience for their ability to rise after defeat or collapse of a business and start a new one with equal vigor and no loss of confidence. They may have good prosperous partners and get financing easily or have money come in from outside sources. They have the ability to handle money and assets. They could have the gift of vocational, rehabilitation, psychological, or medical counseling.

NORTH NODE IN THE NINTH HOUSE OR SAGITTARIUS

Life is involved with an expansion of consciousness. There can be physical, spiritual, or mental travel to expand beyond the reach of the average mind. They may be attracted to spiritual or religious crusades. With the South Node in the third house they may have a great deal of mental activity and a capacity for planning. They may have great success in scientific or literary fields. Their everyday life may be neglected or eccentric. An over concern for brothers and sisters may dissipate their energies. They may have trouble in concentration through an excess of versatility and an over involvement with people in the environment. The mind needs discipline and focus and control of communication. They may have an ease of expression and are highly articulate. They may seek education all through life with a hunger for books and information. They may have a too great reliance on theory and books and become an ivory tower type of person and rely on vicarious experience instead of direct contact with life. They have the danger to over explain and can overkill in persuasion.

North Node in the tenth house or Capricorn

These persons seek a balance between a private and public life. They can be very ambitious and gain a great deal of power. They strive for a place in society through vocation and status. They must prove themselves through achievement and performance. They can achieve fame and become a channel for releasing collective power. They have executive ability and do best in management and administration. These individuals rise in the world over their original status and gain reputation and respect. They prefer the company of other successful people and put great value on worldly performance. Their home lives may be lacking and may have an inability in establishing family ties or to develop roots in any one particular location. They may become a citizen of the world or be footloose. In the opposite vein they could be extremely rooted in family traditions and exclude everyone else and become patriarchal. Another danger is to dissipate inherited power and resources.

North Node in the eleventh house or Aquarius

These individuals must deal with the results of public and professional achievements. They release creative power to do public works for humanitarian concerns. They need group social activities to gain success. They learn to be a friend to everyone but must be careful to not become too popular for their own good. Their personal emotional desires that are egotistical can lead to self undoing. They can take too many risks and have a love of luxury, ostentation, and personal glory. They feel that they can get more of anything and gamble, risking everything. They have a tendency to indulge in plays, sports, or glamour and getting involved with creative and amusing people. They like to entertain and be entertained. They may be always young at heart or negatively they may never grow up. They may be interested in young people and training them in careers. They have a gift for making friends and could develop good business or political connections to help attain their goals. They may join idealistic crusades or may be too much of a joiner. They are altruistic and can be attuned to the spiritual hierarchies. Their capacity for self motivation is being built.

NORTH NODE IN THE TWELFTH HOUSE OR PISCES

These individuals will face and work on problems of a karmic nature. They will have a desire to transcend earthly problems and be reborn into spiritual attitudes in life. They can be involved with healing institutions such as hospitals, prisons, mental or psychological rehabilitation institutions, etc. These people may be reclusive and wish to be left alone. They may have a gift of making large profits in times of crisis like Howard Hughes. Or they may have a life of suffering and illness when too self concerned. They must deal with the end of a cycle of lives and must face situations which will spiritualize the outlook. They must take voluntary self sacrificing choices to repay their karma and be a voluntary martyr. They are capable of making restitution consciously in this life. They can renounce their own ambitions and goals to serve others by sacrificing themselves completely. They can become students of life's mysteries. They can be protected by the spiritual hierarchies and receive eleventh hour protection. They can develop an ease of adjustment to any circumstances, task or problem that confront them.

METHODOLOGY OF NATAL CHART READING

1. Determine the chart ruler.

2. Determine the planetary pattern with focal points.

3. Determine the client's temperament.

4. Determine the client's Soul level, life cycle, and point of self.

5. Study the Sun and its aspects and make notes.

6. Study the Moon and its aspects.

7. Study Mercury and its aspects.

8. Study Venus and its aspects.

9. Study Mars and its aspects.

10. Study Jupiter and its aspects.

11. Study Saturn and its aspects.

12. Study Uranus and its aspects.

13. Study Neptune and its aspects.

14. Study Pluto and its aspects.

15. Study the Moon's Nodes and its aspects.

16. Ask yourself what kind of a past life would create the challenges of this life.

17. Sleep on your question.

18. Receive a picture image of this life.

19. You will have synthesized the meaning of the chart.

20. Talk to the client and helpfully discuss what you have found.

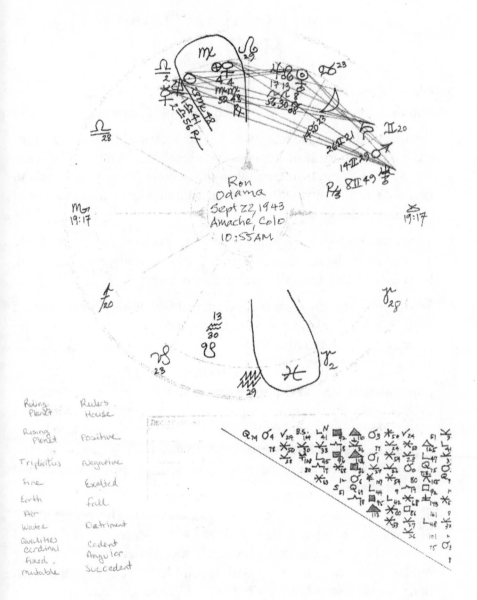

Ron
Odama
Sept 22, 1943
Amache, Colo
10:55 AM

EXAMPLE OF METHODOLOGY
MY CHART

1. Chart ruler – Pluto in Leo in the ninth house. This gives the strong impulse to pursue the study of all higher mind interests.

2. Planetary pattern – Bundle pattern. This shows a highly concentrated one sided pursuit of interests with stable momentum. The leading planet is Uranus in Gemini in the seventh house. This leads to unusual relationships with many varied individuals in an attempt to overcome selfishness.

3. Temperament – Phlegmatic/Choleric polarity with a basic Melancholy. The missing temperament is the Sanguine. Too many lives as a soldier. Lack of musical ability now.

4. Soul level – Moving from the Intellectual Soul to the Consciousness Soul. The life cycle is the quadrant from 63 years to 70 years. The point of self is in the fifth house. A good time to write a book.

5. The Sun – Sun in Virgo in the tenth house intercepted. Working professionally behind the scenes with high humanitarian standards in giving service. Sun in conjunction to Mercury and Neptune in Libra. This gives high idealism, a sense of humor, and thinking in metaphors. All three square to Saturn in the eighth house in Gemini. This brings practicality, logic, method, and patience to speech and thought challenges.

6. The Moon – Moon in Cancer in the eighth house. This brings a love of traditions, home and family, devotion to ideals and nurturing of others. There is also a strong interest in racial issues and justice. The mother's influence is strong with a quintile to the Sun in the tenth house and a septile to Venus in the tenth house in Virgo.

7. Mercury – Mercury in Libra in the eleventh house, not intercepted. This can be interpreted as a focus on group dynamics in making consensus decisions. Because of the square aspect from Saturn, practicality must be balanced by principle. Mercury rises after the Sun, retrograde in conjunction to the Sun and Neptune which gives a highly impressionable and subjective thinking of a historical perspective.

8. Venus – Venus in Virgo in the tenth house close to the Midheaven. Professional affairs are favored by mentors who are very precise and knowledgeable. Since Venus rules the seventh house cusp, it denotes a partner that is a professional involved with beauty and service. My wife had a beauty shop and was always devoted to cosmetics, hair styling, etc. I always tried as a Waldorf teacher to include the arts and music in the teaching of all academics.

9. Mars – Mars in Gemini in the seventh house, conjunction to Uranus and sextile to Pluto, North Node, and Jupiter in Leo in the ninth house. There has been an attempt to delve into the depths of understanding the needs of students through astrology and Anthroposophy. There has also been challenges to overcome anger and willful actions and speech. I have had to learn diplomacy and tact.

10. Jupiter – Jupiter in Leo in the ninth house. This has led me into the study of all philosophies and how they can be practically applied in teaching of children. The pursuit of knowledge and wisdom has been all encompassing.

11. Saturn – Saturn in Gemini in the eighth house. This has led to a lifelong evaluation of external and internal expectations to find truth in racial, tribal, national, economic, and political issues. I taught black, Hispanic, Caucasian, Asian, American Indian, Hawaiian students and all mixtures in a search for truth versus political correctness. Since there is a square of Saturn to the triple conjunction of Sun, Neptune, and Mercury in the tenth house there is a sensitivity to political justice.

12. Uranus – Uranus in Gemini in the seventh house, conjunction to Mars, sextile to Pluto conjunct North Node in Leo in the ninth house, and trine to Sun in Virgo in the tenth conjunct to Neptune and Mercury in Libra in the cusp of the tenth and eleventh houses has led to challenges in my professional life in dealing with authority, group decisions, and the application of Anthroposophy in teaching and working with colleagues in Waldorf schools.

13. Neptune – Neptune in Libra on the cusp of the eleventh house, conjunction to Sun and Mercury, square to Saturn in Gemini in the eighth house, sextile to Pluto in Leo in the ninth house, and trine to Uranus in Gemini in the seventh house has brought idealism, sensitivity, and criticalness in the depiction of spiritual values in art,

drama, poetry, film, music etc. Also it brings the attempt to work in groups by building consensus.

14. Pluto – Pluto in Leo in the ninth house, conjunction to the North Node and sextile to Uranus in Gemini in the seventh, and Sun, Neptune and Mercury conjunct in Virgo and Libra on the cusp of the eleventh house and acting as the midpoint of the defining trine of my bundle, and ruler of my chart has brought a focus to my search for truth in universality.

15. North Node – North Node in Leo in the ninth house conjunct to Jupiter, and sextile to Mars in Gemini in the seventh house has helped me to work spiritually in working with my students, individualizing their instruction, and penetrating into their diagnostic and prescriptive needs, strengths and weaknesses and educational plans on a daily basis.

16. Chiron and Part of Fortune – Chiron conjunct Part of Fortune in Virgo in the tenth house conjunct Venus has led me into teaching as a profession bringing me great satisfaction.

This concludes my example of the methodology of how to read a natal chart. I hope it is instructive to you in your work. Good luck!

APPENDIX: THE TEMPERAMENTS
HOW TO LOVINGLY HANDLE ADULTS

MELANCHOLIC

- Treat kindly. Ask questions to take charge. This cuts their lengthy talk of woe short. This allows them to talk themselves dry.

- Make claims upon their friendship. Ask them to do favors for you. This allows them to think of the needs of others and forget themselves.

PHLEGMATIC

- To arouse interest to action – sow seeds and keep tending. Make the "new" ordinary by repeated attempts at familiarization. "So and so has been using such and such for a long time." Be sure so and so is considered respectable, and such and such has quality and taste.

- Provide the opportunity to copy or imitate then make improvements. Praise accomplishments and make alterations without comment.

- Never do anything to upset the balance of normal routines of existence. Surprises could lead to drastic, tragic reactions.

SANGUINE

- Be kind and not disagreeable. Don't lose self-control and become angry. If you force confessions they will lie.

- Don't treat them as equals, but as inferiors. Love to follow cholerics.

- Act with strength of character, being non-impressionable to sharp criticism.

- Give tasks that can be completed quickly.

CHOLERIC

- Treat with love and kind words. Appeal to sense of honor and fairness.

- Must never cry or show self-pity. No clinging vines. No uncertainty.

- Gang up on them when they have been too egotistical. Show results of indiscretions.

- Go to them first before time limits are exceeded to explain problems. Have a plan of action.

- Ask them to help you! They can't stand suffering when they can help.

- Don't tell them they remind you of others or that their behaviors are familiar.

The Temperaments
How to Lovingly Handle Children

Melancholic

- Tell stories of pain and suffering from your own life and experiences of those you know.

- Give examples of how work and service brought transformation into people's lives and how love triumphs.

- Never allow a melancholic child to become a tyrant through complaints and demands.

- Ask them questions about their concerns and let them talk themselves dry.

- Ask them to do service for others or pets.

Phlegmatic

- Non-interest in the world must be awakened through the interests of others.

- Encourage them to copy and imitate and later to make innovations.

- Don't criticize or they will be offended and crawl into a shell.

- Quietly make corrections and leave them alone. They don't want to stand out from the group.

- Let them be helpers and take care of details. They want to be dependable.

- Allow events to occur where apathy is appropriate.

Sanguine

- Be loving and help the child to find an interest that draws his/her attention on a long term basis.

- Be reactive to criticism or crises. Child searches for a personality that is non-reactive (Choleric.)

- Never treat them as equals, but tell them their choices.

- Don't confront, as this leads to lying, non-reliability or superficiality.

- Give tasks that can be accomplished quickly.

CHOLERIC

- Be masterful and not show insecurity or indecisiveness.

- Give difficult tasks that require strength and perseverance to accomplish. Tasks may have trivial results compared to efforts exerted.

- Confront by showing pain or suffering that were created by their words or actions. Allow them to cool off first.

- Appeal to sense of justice and honor.

	Choleric	Sanguine	Phlegmatic	Melancholic
Physical Appearance	short, stocky, bull-necked, upright	slender, elegant, well-balanced	big, fleshy, rotund	Large, bony, heavy-limbed with bowed head
Walk	firm, digging heels in ground	light, tripping on the toes	rolling, ambling (steam-roller)	Slow with drooping, sliding gait
Eyes	energetic, active	dancing, lively	sleepy, often half-closed	tragic, mournful
Gestures	short, abrupt	graceful, lively	slow, deliberate	drooping
Manner of Speaking	sharp, emphatic, deliverate, to the point	eloquent, with flowery language	ponderous, logical, clear	hesitating, halting, not completing sentences
Relationships	friendly as long as recognized leader	friendly to all, fickle, changeable	friendly but reserved, impassive	poor, has sympathy only with fellow-sufferers
Habits	must jolly everyone else along	is flexible, has not fixed habits	likes routine, has set habits	likes solitary occupations
Food	enjoys spicy oods, well-prepared	nibbles, likes nicely prepared things	eats good square meals of anything	is finicky, likes sweet things
Dress	likes something individual and outstanding	likes anything new, anything colorful	has a conservative taste	chooses drab clothes, is difficult to please
Powers of Observation	observes what is of interest but forgets	notices everything and forgets everything	observes and remembers exactly when sufficiently awake	observes little but remembers it
Memory	poor	like a sieve	good concerning the world	good concerning self
Interests	the world, self and the future	the immediate present	the present without getting involved	self and the past
Attitudes	commanding, aggressive, eventually understanding	kind, understanding, sympathetic	discerning, objective	egoistical, vindictive, self-sacrificing in cases of suffering
Disposition	boasting, enthusiastic, generous, intolerant, impatient, gambling	changeable, superficial, unreliable, kind, impatient, friendly	faithful, stable, methodical, lethargic, self-contented, trustworthy, motherly	self-absorbed, easily depressed, fearful, moody, tyrannical, helpful, artistic
Paintings/Drawings (Childrens')	volcanoes, precipices with self-overcoming obstacles, strong colors	lots of bright colors, movement and detail	bland, uninteresting, unfinished in appearance	strong, harmonious colors, attempts too much detail

This chart excerpted from: ❋❋❋

Classic Fairy Tale Symbology:

Characters from "All kinds of Fur" by Brothers Grimm

Old King	ego before self-consciousness
New King	Divine Ego
Old Queen	soul before self-consciousness
New Queen	consciousness soul/spirit self
Prince	young ego
Princess	young soul
Orphan	must find one's own path
Chef	life experiences
Golden Hair	atavistic clairvoyance
Golden, silvery, starry dresses	true astral body
Cloak of furs	astral characteristics of the animal kingdom
Forest	life's scary path
Hollow tree	sense-world thinking
Nutshell	skull
Pudding	astral temptations

THREEFOLD SOUL EXPRESSION:
THINKING, FEELING & WILLING

3 Foldness

The Soul can express itself through
  Thinking, Feeling, + Willing.
Nerve Sense   Rhythmic   Metabolis Limbs
  Head   Heart, lung   Hand

inspiration   intuition
              Feeling
Thinking   imagination
                         willing
feeling

willing

Signs

Mutable	Fixed	Cardinal
♊	♉	♈
♍	♌	♋
♐	♏	♎
♓	♒	♑
Wisdom	Love	Will

Houses

Cadent	Succeedent	Active
3, 6, 9, 12	2, 5, 8, 11	1, 4, 7, 10
Disperse	Concentrate	Generate

TWO FACES OF EVIL

Two Faces of Evil!

Lucifer (Devil) Light	Christ the Redeemer	Ahriman (Satan) Darkness
Chinese incarnation 3000 BC	Will appear in the etheric (2nd Coming)	American incarnation
Desires man to abandon the earth	Good, True + Beautiful	Desires to make man earth bound by denying the Spirit. Materialism
Spiritualism on a low order	Judgement + Discernment	Works on the intellectual Soul
Works on the astral body + Sentient Soul / Passions, urges + desires	Morality	Counteracted by karma
Counteracted by - illness, pain + Suffering		Mechanistic view of the cosmos devoid of the Spirit
Personal egoism reach Nirvana for Self		Probabilities (mathematics) Prove hypotheses
Blind faith		Life events happen by chance
False idealism + spirituality		Lies, half truths, deceit
		Proliferation of knowledge and communication of facts without truth + reality
		Promotes belief that all answers Can be found by measurement
		Promotes nationalism, tribalism Sectarianism